ROCKWELL LECTURES

The Rice Institute

Religion and American Democracy

BY

ROY F. NICHOLS

LOUISIANA STATE UNIVERSITY PRESS

BATON ROUGE

1959

By Roy F. Nichols

The Democratic Machine, 1850–54
Syllabus for History of Civilization (joint author)
America Yesterday and Today (with Charles A. Beard
  and W. C. Bagley)
Growth of American Democracy (with Jeannette P.
  Nichols)
The Republic of the United States: A History (with
  Jeannnette P. Nichols)
A Short History of American Democracy (with Jean-
  nette P. Nichols)
Franklin Pierce: Young Hickory of the Granite Hills
Disruption of the American Democracy
The Historical Study of Anglo-American Democracy
Advance Agents of American Destiny

Copyright 1959 by
Louisiana State University Press
Library of Congress Catalog Card No.: 59–9085
Manufactured in the United States of America by J. H. Furst Co.
Baltimore, Maryland

FOREWORD

There has always been a close association between government and religion, for from each men receive the rules by which their lives are governed. Government and religion supply the leadership without which most men are not willing to live. As these rules and ways of thinking about conduct are basic influences in shaping men's behavior, their definition is a determining factor in thinking about society and themselves. The thoughts and expressions which men use about their politico-religious life are distinctive culture characteristics which mark the different national or racial groups and serve as rallying points of propaganda in culture conflicts.

In view of the prevailing controversies and rivalries in the world it is appropriate to attempt a definition of the relationship between religion and American democracy. Such a definition is here presented as nearly as possible in the words used by the leaders and formulators of the ideas and by the generations of citizens of the United States whose thoughts and actions have been controlled by them.

v

PREFACE

These lectures were delivered at The Rice Institute, in Houston, Texas, under the auspices of the Rockwell Fund. I am privileged to express my gratitude to my gracious hosts, President and Mrs. William V. Houston, Professor and Mrs. William H. Masterson, and their associates in the History Department. I acknowledge with pleasure my indebtedness to Dr. Elizabeth M. Geffen and Professor Masterson for their critical reading of the manuscript. My thanks are particularly due to Dr. Robert T. Handy of Union Theological Seminary, a perceptive theologian who saved this layman from a number of blunders. The errors, theological and otherwise, that may have survived, however, are my sole responsibility.

ROY F. NICHOLS

The University of Pennsylvania
February, 1959

vii

TABLE OF CONTENTS

Religion and American Democracy

The Democracy of American Religion

THE age of discovery which brought America within European ken was likewise an era of religious reorientation, the Reformation. The institutions of the new society beyond the seas were influenced in a significant number of American colonies by the religious searchings which marked the English phase of the Christian reordering. The Reformation in England stimulated democratic developments in the political evolution of some of the new societies, and it likewise brought government and religion into a new and somewhat altered relationship which has not been too well understood. This relationship may be said to have become, paradoxically, all the closer because it appeared in a sense to have been destroyed.

American society was formed by people from European cultures in which the tradition of the close relation, almost unity, of church and state was ages old. Those who would rule had long ago discovered that it was advantageous to have the sanction and support of those who could invoke the favor of the divine, and whose religious authority controlled the behavior of the men and women to whom they administered the sacraments of the Christian Church. The Kings

3

of England worked in close association with the clergy, some of whom served as administrators, diplomats, and keepers of the rolls. They were ever present in the royal privy council and shared in the rule of the realm. Clerics were likewise the educators. And they became wealthy property holders, cared for the poor, dispensed justice, and at times led armies in the field. They came to their greatest influence at the time of the Crusades, and their power is illustrated by the fact that the king acknowledged himself, once at least, to be a vassal of the Roman Pontiff. But America was created at a time when there was a great and fundamental change taking place in the basic social ordering of Europe. In fact, the discovery of America and the establishment of a new order in this New World were phases of this great transformation.

The fourteenth, fifteenth, and sixteenth centuries were to be ages of unusual human activity, of adventure and discovery. It is common practice to think of the climax of these achievements in terms of daring voyages across unknown seas and the discovery of continents. But it may also be thought of in terms of adventures in human relations and in the discovery of man himself. It was the age when man oriented himself as an individual, an age in which he emerged from the mass. Consequently, it was an era of religious enterprise. Man searched out for himself a new relationship with God, he gained a new sense of

4

his dignity and power, and he found liberty. In finding himself and his freedom, man likewise freed his imagination. So magnificent a concept as a society of free men enjoying liberty, of men who knew God and were equal in His sight—this concept stirred men to dreams of a new and perfected society. But such dreams could not be realized in ancient societies; they demanded a new world, and lo! a new world was at hand.

One of the significant indications of this new outlook was expression of discontent with the prevailing operation of church and state, particularly the former. By the fourteenth century the forms of worship had become set in formalized liturgy, conducted by a clerical hierarchy in what was becoming to many an unsatisfying routine fashion. These clergy, often unprepossessing and even corrupt, were acting as the keepers of a mystery and not as those opening the pages of the Book of Life. The priesthood was keeping God from men; even God's word was imprisoned in Latin. But men fired with a new zeal would not be denied. Wyclif and the Lollards paved the way and sought to open the Bible to the people. They were sternly suppressed by the united force of state and church, but the spirit of these searchers persisted, and when Erasmus came to Cambridge, and when the doctrines of Luther were brought across the North

Sea, there were those who were ready to intensify the search.

This new yearning for God by individuals who wished to read the Scriptures was but one of various trends which made it possible for Henry VIII and his government to nationalize the English Church by renouncing allegiance to Rome, to sequester its monastic property, and to organize the sees, dioceses, and parishes into an Anglican Church of which the king would be the head. In his new role he appointed the prelates and continued to employ them as ministers of state. Seemingly the relationship of crown and church was closer than ever, but in fact, the tie was in the process of loosening.

The sixteenth century was, in truth, a time in which men were increasingly jealous of their own religious opinions, of their independence of religious thought. They were also disturbed by the worldliness characteristic of the Renaissance. When Erasmus taught in Cambridge, and when the doctrines of Luther, emphasizing salvation of sinful man through faith in God's grace, began to be discussed in the colleges and inns of that University, there was a response from an obscure underground remnant of the Lollards, the "secret multitude of true professors," the Known Men. When Henry VIII, as newly proclaimed head of the Church, authorized the Oxford scholar, Tyndale, to translate the Bible into English, the way to individual communion with God became easier.[1]

The more men read, thought about, and discussed religion, the more various became their ideas. The teachings of John Calvin were brought over from the continent and concepts of total depravity and pre-destination were set up unmodified by Luther's more comfortable doctrine of salvation through faith, and so strongly stated as to stimulate Arminius to pro-claim the infinity of God's grace. Besides differences over intricate doctrinal points there was controversy over methods of worship. The new Anglican Church continued many of the Roman liturgical forms, where-as no inconsiderable number of those whose minds had been opened wished to purify the service and these Puritans called for a didactic and polemical form of worship in which preaching should be the central part. Likewise there naturally arose disputa-tion over the form of church government and the relation of church and state. The episcopal form of rule by the bishops was disputed, and two principal alternatives advocated: a presbyterian rule by clergy and elders meeting in representative synods, and a congregational polity in which each parish would govern itself.

The politics of this sixteenth century were com-plicated by the personalities of those involved in the reigns of Henry VIII, Edward VI, Mary, and Elizabeth; and the domestic changes and foreign rivalries so characteristic of the age made these questions of ritual and religious order issues as burning as were doctrinal controversies. The sovereign was head of the Church, and any questioning of the sovereign's acts in the matter of church government or of laws enacted in the sovereign's name in the same category could be denominated heresy or treason. Men might be burned at the stake, drawn and quartered, or made to abjure the realm as punishment. Controversy reached a height in the reigns of Elizabeth and her successor, James I, when clergymen and their parishes began to go in various ecclesiastical directions in designs of church polity. The main body was only stiffened in its loyalty to the Anglican order, but Puritan, Presbyterian, and Congregational ideas were drawing many away and the latter were taking stands which meant that their allegiance to sovereign and bishop in matters of religion might appear to be renounced. For such there were penalties, legal and social.

What had happened was the introduction of a new concept of ecclesiastico-political association. Local units which were part religious and part civil government—namely the parish, managed by priest, wardens and vestry—were assuming an independence of central authority which would be resisted and, if possible, punished by this same power. In the latter years of

Elizabeth's reign some determined to maintain their ideals of independence and to escape imprisonment or worse by leaving England. Under the lead of Cambridge graduates this move began. As early as 1593 a Congregation in London decided to migrate to Holland and settle in Amsterdam; somewhat later the group at Gainsborough in Lincolnshire followed them. Most famous of the groups to migrate was the congregation at Scrooby in Nottinghamshire, which went to Holland in 1609 and established itself at Leyden, under the leadership of its Cambridge trained pastor, John Robinson. He was a man of unusual vision who sought to lead his flock out of the morass of doctrinal controversy, particularly away from the area of conflict between Lutheran and Calvinist. As Robinson put it: "Luther and Calvin were precious shining lights in their times, yet God did not reveal his whole will to them . . . I am very confident that the Lord hath more truth and light yet to break forth out of His Holy Word." [2] Robinson's followers were taught to search for this light.

The congregation at Scrooby had thus undertaken, in England, to order their own ways as a religious association and in Holland they continued so to do as a democratic society, yet within another jurisdiction, the Dutch Republic. However, their situation did not satisfy them, primarily because they were Englishmen and they wished their children to grow

9

up in English ways and on English soil. But the Stuart climate was no more favorable to their independence than the Tudor had been. If they would return to English jurisdiction it must be to the American colonies. So they negotiated with one of the English colonizing corporations and through the manager-director of the London Company, Sir Edmund Sandys, whose elder brother had dwelt in Scrooby, they made a contract. Those in the congregation who were able and willing to go were not enough, so through their business associates in London they sought both cash and recruits. Finally they achieved both, and under patent from the London Company set sail in 1620 for the shores of Virginia.

It was a tempestuous autumn, and the winds were contrary; perhaps the navigator was not too skillful. At any rate, when two months later the 102 pilgrims found themselves worn but, thank God, in sight of land, they realized two things. First, they were not where they should be; and second, being outside the limits of the London Company's possessions, they had no legal right to " settle." But settle they would, despite the fact that there was unfortunate division among the little company. When the final decisions had been made, only thirty-five like-minded in religion with the Scrooby church had been prepared to go, and they were but a minority of the 102. Already there was disaffection and now with no valid license how stood they? The forty-one responsible voting members were almost evenly divided, but nineteen of them were Congregational planners. They were going soon to land on terra firma, they hoped, but before doing so the leaders persuaded all that they must have some form of government which of necessity must be of their own creation. Once more they must act independently. It is significant that their first decision was to create a political instrument with democratic implications.

As a congregation they were familiar with church covenants, so it was but natural that they should put their agreement to organize a self-governing society in such form and in such language: " In the Name of God " they did "by these Presents, solemnly and mutually in the Presence of God and one another, covenant and combine [themselves] together into a civil Body Politick, for [their] Ordering and Preservation . . . and by Virtue [of this covenant did] enact, constitute and frame, such just and equal Laws . . . unto which [they promised] all due Submission and Obedience." [3] Thus in the words of their historian they "joined themselves in the fellowship of the Gospel, to walk in all [God's] ways, made known, or to be made known . . . whatever it should cost them, the Lord assisting them." [4] Having thus covenanted and agreed on shipboard, they eventually landed and founded their new society untrammeled by those forms of the old order to which they could not in conscience conform. They established Plymouth Colony.

As the Stuart dynasty advanced into the seventeenth century it proved less favorable to any pretensions of ecclesiastical independence. Not only were Congregationalists in danger of legal action and punishment, but the outwardly conforming Puritans came into increasing disadvantage. A number of substantial men, some of them country gentlemen in the southwest of England, found themselves harrassed by mounting difficulties. Not only were they in political jeopardy, but they must meet social disfavor at a time when inflation was forcing them to face the lowering of their standard of living under now inadequate fixed incomes. They became increasingly convinced that the Anglican Church and English society were corrupt and sinful, and they yearned for some opportunity to create for themselves a Wilderness Zion. By 1629 one of the foremost of them became " verily persuaded, God will bringe some heavye Affliction upon this lande, and that speedylye "; but he took comfort, for he believed " If the Lord seeth it wilbe good for us, he will provide a shelter and a hidinge place for us and others, as a Zoar for Lott, Sarephtah for his prophet; if not, yet he will not forsake us." [5]

These Puritans were always willing to cooperate with the Almighty in any plans for their better ordering, so they began to prepare for their own Zion. Being men of greater wealth and influence than their Congregational contemporaries, they planned on a larger scale and of their own means. They would go to America, but not as a congregation; rather they would become stockholders in a corporation of their own chartering. Then they would migrate as a company, taking their charter with them, and set up their headquarters in America, in the region commonly called Massachusetts Bay. In this area it would be the duty of the governor and such of the Board of Directors and stockholders as might be assembled in general meeting " to make, ordeine, and establishe all Manner of wholesome and reasonable . . . Lawes . . . for the directing . . . of all other Matters and Thinges, whereby our said People . . . may be soe religiously, peaceablie, and civilly governed, as their good Life and orderlie Conversacon, maie wynn and incite the Natives of [the] Country to the Knowledg and Obedience of the onlie tru God and Savior of Mankinde and the Christian Fayth which in . . . the Adventurers free Profession, is the principall Ende of this Plantacion." [6] Shortly thereafter the leaders of this group met together at Cambridge, the source of so much of their inspiration, and there bound themselves " in the word of a Christian and in the presence of God who is the searcher of all hearts, that we will so really endeavour the execution of his worke, as by God's assistance we will be ready . . . in our persons . . . to embarke." [7]

In due season a great company—more than a thousand in fourteen ships—set sail, and as they lost sight of the homeland they had with them the comfort of the text for Rev. Mr. Cotton's last sermon on shore. " Moreover I will appoint a place for my people Israel, and will plant them, that they may dwell in a place of their own, and move no more; neither shall the children of wickedness afflict them any more, as beforetime." [8] They were on their way to a new Canaan in the wilderness beyond the sea.

The New Canaan which these Massachusetts Bay adventurers founded was much more flourishing and numerous in population than the small Plymouth to the southeast. But its success and prosperity did not bring it peace. Those who were its leaders were dedicated to the idea of a Puritan Zion and it was not long before the corporate structure had substituted for it a rule of the priests and elders. They were not to break with the Church of England in any striking official way, but they were to be non-Separatist Congregationalists. In fact, they were going in the direction of the Congregational Pilgrims—though not at first along a democratic path. This phase Governor

Winthrop distrusted; he could find no warrant for democracy in the Scriptures.

Those who believed in election and damnation could scarcely think much of equality. Instead of Congregational democracy, the rule of a Puritan theocracy was to be substituted, and by the end of the first year only church members were permitted to vote. Ministers and elders kept stern watch and ward. They frowned on the Rev. Roger Williams and Mistress Ann Hutchinson in such fashion as to disturb Rev. Mr. Thomas Hooker. To dedicated men and women, such as Williams, Mrs. Hutchinson, and Hooker, power was being concentrated in undesired fashion in the hands of the ecclesiastical leaders in Boston. The Governor and the Board of Directors residing for the most part in this growing wilderness metropolis, were, in the name of religion and for the purpose of crushing out sin and defeating the wiles of the devil, creating a strait-laced autocracy which was constantly interfering with the lives and thoughts of the people and with the independence of the burgeoning towns multiplying in the hinterland.

These difficulties stimulated two tendencies which were to be characteristic of American democracy. The original plan of running the colony through magistrates—in effect chosen for a long term and replenished only by themselves—whose authority should rest on the consent of such " freemen " or stockholders who might take the trouble to attend the annual meetings in Boston, was not pleasing. The increasing number of growing towns were not taking kindly to the assumption of command and taxing power by the Boston theocrats and they were quick to protest. They were of the same spirit as the Pilgrims and the Massachusetts Bay leaders, and by 1634 they were able to secure the acceptance of the idea of representation in law making. The towns were authorized to send representatives of their own choosing to the " general court " in Boston where they sat with the Governor and the Assistants as a legislature.

This step toward democracy was notable, but not altogether satisfying. The theocratic governor and his assistants, much under the influence of the Boston clergy, could negate the will of the representatives of the towns, and discontent continued to simmer. Therefore a second American device was employed. The discontented, as the Pilgrims and the Massachusetts Bay Company had set the example, would move on and attempt to improve on their handiwork— would again create societies. Part of this activity was involuntary. The gifted young clergyman, Roger Williams, ever a " seeker," was banished because he questioned the rule of the Boston elders. Mrs. Hutchinson, who was the first American lady to concern herself with public affairs and who furthermore questioned certain male judgments (even creating a wilderness salon where the wisdom of the theocrats was challenged) likewise was expelled. These and various of the "otherwise minded" dauntlessly went forth, Williams even in the snow of winter, and established Rhode Island as a refuge for those who would not conform. They raised the standard of religious liberty over their tiny republic.

Almost simultaneously with Williams' effort another hive of settlements was set up by those who left of their own free will. The enterprising had been heartened by tidings of the fertile soil of the Connecticut River Valley, and thither with the reluctant consent of the Bay Colony authorities various groups began to move. A series of town migrations took place, most notable of which was the move of the Newtown parish (Cambridge) under the lead of its pastor, the Rev. Mr. Thomas Hooker who did not see eye to eye with the Boston theocrats and who was more charitable in admitting members to the church. The result was a series of settlements, Hartford, Windsor, Weathersfield, and Saybrook, who, when they had established themselves, met to create a federation of Puritan towns. This they were going to do independently, without reference to the King. They framed their purpose thus: "Where a people are gathered together the word of God requires that to mayntayne the peace and union of such a people there should be an orderly and decent Government established according to God, to order and dispose of the affayres of the people at all seasons as occasion shall require." Therefore these Connecticut River towns would " assotiate and conioyne our selves to be as one Publike State or Commonwealth; and doe . . . enter into . . . Confederation togather, to mayntayne and presearve the liberty and purity of the gospell of our Lord Jesus which we now professe, as also the disciplyne of the Churches, which according to the truth of the said gospell is now practised amongst us." So they subscribed themselves as the creators of their gospel republic which, through representatives of the towns, should make its own laws and have as its head a governor " alwayes a member of some approved congregation." [9] Here again this urge for congregational and community independence had stirred not only a migration but the creation of a federated republic—the first germ of the process which came to such effective climax in 1789.

A third move of this type had even stronger religious motivation and marked probably the most radical of the contributions of religion to American democracy. A London clergyman and Oxford man, the Rev. Mr. John Davenport, found himself in such difficulties with Archbishop Laud that he could no longer remain in England. After a brief sojourn in Holland, where he was equally unhappy, he re-

turned to London. There he persuaded a wealthy
parishioner in his former church, St. Stephens (the
man had also once been his public school chum), to
finance a venture in America. Davenport would
create a religious colony and be its pastor; Eaton
would develop its trading potential. In 1637 they
took over a party, spent a winter in Boston, where
they found morals and religious doctrine not strict
enough, and then set out for the western part of
Connecticut, by-passing the confederated towns.
Here on the shore of Long Island Sound they founded
their "New Haven." Here they created a model
biblical state.

All the "free planters" gathered together in a
covenant meeting as it were, "to consult about settling
civill Government according to God . . . . After
solemne invocation of the name of God in prayer
[for] the presence and help of his sperrit, and grace
in those weighty businesses . . . the establishment of
such civill order as might be most pleasing unto God
. . . for the better inableing them to discern the minde
of God and to agree accordingly," they entered into
discussion of means. The Rev. Mr. Davenport asked
them "whether the Scriptures doe holde forth a perfect rule for the direction and government of all men
in all duties which they are to performe to God and
men . . . ? " They all raised their hands in affirmation.
They further agreed that in all things connected with

government they would be ordered by those rules which the Scripture held forth. All then confessed a desire to be church members and agreed that only church members should be magistrates and officers. Nominations of twelve men then were made, and only one was objected to. He had taken an "excessive rate for meale which he sould to one of Pequanack in his need." This he "confessed with griefe and declared thatt haveing beene smitten in heart and troubled in his conscience, he [had] restored such a part of the price back againe with confession of his sin to the party as he thought himself bound to doe." He was forgiven but as it was "feared thatt the report of the sin was heard farther than the report of his satisfaction, a course was concluded on to make the satisfaction known to as many as heard of the sinn." [10] This covenant of 1639 served New Haven as its constitution for a Bible commonwealth, the laws of which were drawn from Scripture, for a quarter of a century. In these years a number of like-minded believers in theocracy had founded other churches and towns in the vicinity and on nearby Long Island. Then a change in the English government caused some disquiet. The Stuarts were restored and Charles II and his brother, the Duke of York, gave much concern to America. One of their decisions was to consolidate some of the colonies, and New Haven and its satellites found themselves placed under Connecticut's jurisdiction. To some this was disturbing. And then came divine inspiration.

One of the American projects of the Stuarts had been the conquest of New Amsterdam. When that was consummated the Duke of York placed New Jersey in the hands of Sir George Carteret and Lord Berkeley. Sir George sent his brother over to promote settlement and the brother sent agents to New England to offer advantageous terms of settlement. These agents visited the New Haven towns in the midst of their discontent. Some citizens, particularly of the towns of Milford, Guilford, and Branford, were ready to move. They did not think the Connecticut towns sufficiently strict in their theocracy. So some of these citizens, particularly the Minister and Congregation of Milford, would do as the Pilgrims, the Massachusetts Bay Company, Roger Williams, Thomas Hooker, and John Davenport had done. They would move again and make a new effort to create their Biblical Commonwealth under the lead of the Rev. Mr. Abraham Pierson and Captain Robert Treat. However, they did not project a colony; they would be content to establish one town within another jurisdiction.

These migrants " according to fundamentals mutually agreed upon, do desire to be of one heart and consent, through God's blessing with one hand they may endeavor the carrying on of spiritual concern-

ments as also civil and town affairs according to God
and a Godly government." The system that they
subscribed was based upon certain Scriptural pas-
sages:

"Take you wise men, and understanding, and
known, among your tribes, and I will make them
rulers over you." (Deut. 1, 13)

"Moreover, thou shalt provide out of all the
people able men, such as fear God, men of truth,
hating covetousness; and place such over them,
to be rulers of thousands, and rulers of hundreds,
rulers of fifties, and rulers of tens." (Ex. 18, 21)

"Thou shalt in anywise set him king over
thee, whom the Lord thy God shall choose: one
from among thy brethren shalt thou set king over
thee; thou mayest not set a stranger over thee,
which is not thy brother." (Deut. 15, 17)

"And their nobles shall be of themselves and
their governors shall proceed from the midst of
them." (Jer. 30, 31)

With these principles firmly fixed in mind they
agreed that " none shall be admitted freemen or free
Burgesses . . . but such Planters as are members of
some or other of the Congregational Churches nor
shall any but such be chosen to Magistry [to legislature, to judiciary, or to military command]. Nor
shall any But such Church Members have any Vote

in . . . elections." They all agreed "with Care and Diligence [to] provide for the maintenance of the purity of Religion professed in the Congregational Churches." Hereafter only men of Good Carriage and Behaviour " who would agree to pay the amounts for "the Maintainance and allowance agreed upon for the upholding of the settled Ministry and preaching of the word" would be given the vote. Also it was prescribed that if "any shall come into us or arise up amongst us that shall willingly or wilfully disturb us in our Peace and Settlements, and especially that would subvert us from the true Religion and worship of God, and cannot or will not keep their opinions to themselves " [11] they shall be caused to leave the company and depart hence. Thus was established Newark, New Jersey, in fact a migrant congregation locating within the already established jurisdiction of Sir George Carteret's colony of East Jersey.

Thus between 1593 and 1666 the resolution of religious people had been so strong that they left England, dared the angry deep, struggled for their New Canaans and, when they found them not, went onward to new endeavor, still trusting in God's help to lead them to a promised land. Everywhere they went they established towns and confederacies in which, despite a predilection for a theocratic rule, a self-governing town emerged where men of good carriage and behavior, a surprisingly large proportion, participated in the common affairs; and if minister and elders did somewhat greatly influence their actions, they spoke in God's name to His children.

Another series of religious interests in America soon followed the creation of the Congregational ecclesiastical foundation in New England and the town at Newark, East Jersey. In England a new group of believers, the Society of Friends called Quakers, was coming into greater spiritual and economic power. These men and women formed a democratic religious society without priests, in which all shared God's direction—revealed to them by the Inner Light and guided by conscience—and undertook to live by a law of love. All men were to be friends and live under a friendly persuasion. They would not recognize civil authority in religious matters: all men were equal in the sight of God. They would not fight, and would not go to law or take oaths: they would arbitrate and rely on men's solemn promises. These Friends had first come to New England in 1656 where Massachusetts had banished them as undesirables but Rhode Island had welcomed them. They established their first yearly meeting there in 1661 and by 1672 they held the chief posts in the government of the colony. Their great apostle, George Fox, together with the wealthy and socially prominent William Penn, and other substantial and earnest citizens, had in the meantime looked out upon the world and found the ordinary temper of society wanting in any spirit akin to God's holy laws. Fox came to America in that same year, 1672. He was inspired by what he found and returned zealous to persuade his fellow Friends to go to this new world where they might well found a superior society.

So, at this time, a group of Quakers approached the owner of the great estate of West Jersey and bought, through an agent, the southwestern half of New Jersey, originally granted to Lord Berkeley. William Penn became interested in this area and helped to frame a scheme of government which would provide a place where freedom of conscience would be assured and Quakers enabled to establish the law of love. But there were others involved who did not share these ideals too heartily, and Penn soon took advantage of the fact that the Crown owed him a heavy debt for money and services supplied by his father, Admiral Penn. He secured a great grant of land in 1681, Pennsylvania, in payment, where he could in truth establish a Holy Experiment of his own design and ordering.

In the concessions issued to the people of New Jersey, Penn and his associates had sought to insure that men were " to understand their liberty as men and Christians, that they may not be brought in bondage, but by their own consent; for we put the power in the people . . . no person to be called in question or molested for his conscience, or for worshipping according to his conscience." [12] Or as it was enacted into law, " All persons living in the Province who confess and acknowledge the one Almighty and Eternal God, and hold themselves obliged in conscience to live peaceably and quietly in a civil society, shall in no way be molested or prejudiced for their religious persuasions and exercise in matters of faith and worship; nor shall they be compelled to frequent and maintain any religious worship, place or ministry whatsoever." [13]

In his planning for Pennsylvania, Penn carried these ideas out more effectively. His religious purpose he described vividly. [For Pennsylvania,] he wrote, " I eyed the Lord in the obtaining of it, and more was I drawn inward to look to Him and to owe it to His hand and power, than to any other way. I have so obtained it, and desire that I may not be unworthy of His love, but do that which may answer His kind providence, and serve His truth and people; that an example may be set up to the nations; there may be room there . . . for such an holy experiment." [14] In this spirit the first laws enacted in Pennsylvania bore the charge: "Whereas, the glory of Almighty God and the good of Mankind is the reason and end of government . . . government in itself is a venerable Ordinance of God." [15] And he gave testimony to the settlers already in Pennsylvania: " I have to let you know that it hath pleased God in His Providence to cast you within my lot and care. It is a business that, though I never undertook before, yet God has given me an understanding of my duty, and an honest mind to do it uprightly . . . you shall be governed by laws of your own making, and live a free . . . people. I shall not usurp the right of any, or oppress his person; God has furnished me with a better resolution, and has given me His grace to keep it." [16]

Penn endeavored to the extent of his ability to make his colony a holy experiment. Men of all creeds and concerns came thither; and, like Rhode Island and Maryland, it was to contribute much to the tendency which prevailed, that self government and religious liberty should be the chief constituents of that new and more enlightened society in the making in America.

Though emphasis has been placed on these vivid religious motivations for colonization on the part of those not conforming to the Church of England, the fact must not be overlooked that religious impulses were effective in certain colonies planted by those of the Anglican persuasion. For that Church also was moved by missionary zeal. When the Crown issued the charter for the London Company's effort in Virginia, this 1606 document contained these words: "We [James I], greatly commending and graciously accepting of [the Company's] Desires for the Furtherance of so noble a Work, which may, by the Providence of Almighty God, hereafter tend to the Glory of his Divine Majesty, in propagating of Christian Religion to such People, as yet live in Darkness and miserable Ignorance of the true Knowledge and Worship of God, and may in time bring the Infidels and Savages, living in those Parts, to human Civility, and to a settled and quiet Government . . . do Give and Grant . . . the Lands . . . for that Colony." [17]

The Rev. Mr. Robert Hunt was chaplain of the first expedition to Jamestown and within a week of the landing of the colonizers he led them in the celebration of the Lords' Supper. The Anglican Church was immediately established and the Governor sought to create some semblance of ecclesiastic state. One of them, Lord Delaware, marched to Church each Sunday in a procession of red-clad soldiers, leading his " counsell " in worship. When the company granted this colony a legislature and the right to make laws, their legal creation was as stern as much of the Puritan legislation to be drafted in New England.

The other colonies chartered by the Crown likewise provided for missionary activity and established the Anglican Church. One of them, Maryland, was planned as a refuge for Catholics and made a notable contribution to the democratic concept of religious freedom, particularly by its Toleration Act of 1649. The last of the colonies, Georgia, was undertaken by a philanthropist, General James Oglethorpe, and designed in part to be a charitable place of rehabilitation for debtors, criminals, and other unfortunates. Religious groups of a variety of persuasions were invited and came thither to settle. Most notable was the fact that for divers seasons John Wesley, the founder of Methodism, and George Whitefield, one of the great preachers of the colonies, ministered there.

In the colonies of Virginia, Maryland, and Georgia, as well as in the Carolinas and New York, the Anglican Church had some sort of established relation with the government along English models. The total effect of establishing the Anglican Church in these colonies and the Congregational meetings in New England and in the one town in New Jersey was the creation along the Atlantic seaboard of North America of a series of entrenched religious elites. These elites ranged from tax-supported Anglican and Congregational churches to the groups in Rhode Island and Pennsylvania where, though there was no establishment, there were those who exercised religious and political predominance, notably the Quakers, and to a lesser extent the religiously dedicated associates of Roger Williams, some of whom were Baptists.

In addition to the established churches there were

numerous other organized religious groups. In New York and Maryland there were the original Dutch Reformed and Roman Catholic churches associated with the founders. Then, beginning in the last quarter of the seventeenth century, new conditions in Europe were sending other bands of religiously minded people to the colonies for a place of spiritual peace. The French Huguenots, after Louis XIV's persecution, the various German sects from the ravaged Palatinate and similar areas, the Scotch-Irish Presbyterians from impoverished Ulster, were groups of great significance. These flocked over and took up their abodes, many of them in the back country of Pennsylvania, Virginia, and the Carolinas. These were people independent in religion and politics and no particular friends to established churches or entrenched aristocracies.

The century or more of establishment together with the coming of these newer religious elements and the fact that there were many new communities being established in the back country, which were jealous of domination by eastern and tide water leaders, meant that there were bound to be dynamic developments in the American society. It was also inevitable that there would be religious changes. These changes were to move in two directions. One was to be intense, traumatic; the other negative, reflecting something of indifference or denial.

The first of these movements was the forerunner of a series of episodes which would occur periodically in later American history. This first of religious revivals, generally referred to as the Great Awakening, reached its height in the 1740's, though a later phase flourished when the Methodists began to be established in the 1760's. Within this great movement were Dutch Reformed, Presbyterian, Baptist, and Congregationalist bodies of believers who were stirred by a wave of powerful preaching by evangelists. They appealed to individuals, to any individual regardless of social status. Sinners must repent, must confess their sins publicly, and demonstrate their conversion to new and righteous modes of life. Thus alone could they be saved from the fires of Hell. Each was a child of God and an object of divine interest. The evangelists labored mightily and indefatigably. Jonathan Edwards, George Whitefield, and many others preached to thousands and many conversions were recorded. There was therefore a great quickening of the spirit, a great stirring of the emotions. In modern phrase many found new status—they were accepted in a society wherein they had hitherto felt inferior or rejected.

These enthusiasms almost inevitably developed schism in some of the churches. Numbers did not like this new excitement, this emotional preaching. It jarred their sense of decorum, of orderly and reverent worship. Also in many instances it brought a new element into the church, a group of more humble people, some of whom undoubtedly would question the right of the established to dominate. The more conservative were referred to on occasion as Old Lights while the more radical were New Lights. The resistance of the conservative to these exhilarating ideas made the radicals more radical and stirred them to question the authority of these conservators of the old religious order. This division over basic principles of conduct was to be increasingly significant.

The second tendency was marked by another questioning of long accepted standards of thought and action. As one group displayed a greater exuberance, a second introduced a new sense of order in the form of a rule of reason. The intellectuals and those who were absorbing something of the new science had much to think about. Again independent individuals were questioning. Newton and Locke had developed a mechanistic concept of the universe and of society, in which nature and man behaved according to immutable, external laws. God had made the universe and man, but at the same time He had formulated laws governing all things. Therefore there was no place for divine intervention, no place for punishment or for reward by a personal God watching the conduct of men. Man's obligation was to learn the universal laws and then follow or reject them. But it was his individual concern and he could expect no love, no pity, no mercy, nor need he fear capricious anger or punishment. Man was not face to face with God, but alone with law and his capacity to comprehend and follow it.

Not only the intellectual among the colonists but many who read little were absorbing these ideas. It was the period of the French and Indian Wars. Many colonial militia men, officers and privates, were associated with British Army contingents. They heard the talk in the officers' messes and fraternized with the soldiers, and from them they discovered some of these rationalistic ideas and their effect on human conduct. They may have been shocked by the religious indifference and the blasphemy of those who reflected the arid winds of British deism, but they were given something to think about, and many were led to question further the orthodox Congregationalism and Presbyterianism to which they were committed. Contact with France and with French prisoners likewise brought in a modicum of Voltaire and Montesquieu, and of French rationalism.

These two religious developments vigorously influenced the course of American democracy. The Great Awakening had unleashed men's minds; had aroused questioning of established orders; had instilled a new sense of individualism and equality. All men were sons of God and equal in His sight. Furthermore these evangelical churches, particularly the Baptists, Presbyterians, and the new Methodists, were widely scattered among the colonies, and their organizations in some instances were intercolonial. They were in effect not colonial, but American. When difficulties developed after the French Wars and relations with Britain became trying, this newly realized individualism and independence would assert itself.

The evolution of rationalism and deism instilled concepts of planning and of orderly procedure. Within the covers of the books of John Locke was neatly deposited the program used in the Glorious Revolution of 1688, and a whole neat theory of rights had been elaborated. This, according to Newton, was an orderly, law-abiding universe and Locke suggested the particular natural laws men should follow to give them their just rights.

It was therefore not too difficult, when the disadvantages of colonial status within the British Empire appeared at the end of the long period of world war, to follow these directions. The world which the Creator had devised was a " candid " one. " Nature's God " had provided Laws for the operation of Nature. All men in this candid world had been " created equal." They were " endowed by their Creator with certain unalienable Rights . . . among these . . . Life, Liberty and the pursuit of Happiness . . . . To secure these rights, Governments are instituted among Men, deriving their just powers from the consent of the governed . . . . Whenever any Form of Government becomes destructive of these ends, it is the Right of the People to alter or to abolish it, and to institute new Government . . . in such form, as to them shall seem most likely to effect their Safety and Happiness." To prove that they had reached the point where they could safely follow this law of Nature laid down by Nature's God they submitted facts " to a candid world." Having proved their case logically and thus having shown that proper and " decent respect to the opinions of mankind " they announced their decision. "Appealing to the Supreme Judge of the world for the rectitude of their intentions," they declared their independence " with a firm reliance on the Protection of Divine Providence." [18] So wrote Thomas Jefferson in the Declaration of Independence.

This fundamental document for the new national venture showed an obvious religious conceptualization. But it was a different one from that which had so influenced the colonial directives. The Jehovah of Israel and the Christ of the Trinity were gone. Here was the Deity of Rationalism who was not appealed to for guidance or protection, but who was called in to witness that His creatures were working under His laws. On these grounds they could justify their faith that they would succeed.

No sooner had this Declaration been issued than the Congress began work on a permanent frame of government designed to establish a perpetual union. This document, The Articles of Confederation, was composed in the midst of war's alarms and it had little concern for the peacetime rights of men. As far as religious interests were concerned, it merely provided that the states enter into a firm league of friendship with each other—for the security of their Liberties—and bind themselves to assist each other, against all force offered to, or attacks made upon them, or any of them, on account of religion. In conclusion they signed the document because " it hath pleased the Great Governor of the World to incline the hearts " of their various legislatures to ratify the instrument.[19]

By the time the nation was ready for a permanent instrument, less than a decade later, however, the delegates gathered to frame it were seemingly unmindful of any religious interest, and the only reference to religion is contained in the provision that " no religious Test shall ever be required as a Qualification to any Office or public Trust under the United States." [20] This omission, representing as it did the rationalistic tendency somewhat popular among the rather youthful public men who dominated the convention, roused a good deal of protest, and the absence of any reference to divine authority was one of the points made against accepting the document. However, it was ratified, and under its provisions George Washington was called to direct its promulgation.

Inauguration Day brought evidence that the authors of the Constitution had not set a precedent in omitting reference to religious guidance. General Washington in the opening sentences of his address to the nation declared that " it would be peculiarly improper to omit in this first official act my fervent supplications to that Almighty Being who rules over the universe, who presides in the councils of nations, and whose providential aids can supply every human defect, that His benediction may consecrate to the liberties and happiness of the people of the United States a Government instituted by themselves for these essential purposes, and may enable every instrument employed in its administration to execute with success the functions allotted to his charge." In tendering this

> homage to the Great Author of every public and private good, I assure myself that it expresses your sentiments not less than my own . . . . No people can be bound to acknowledge and adore the Invisible Hand which conducts the affairs of men more than those of the United States. Every step by which they have advanced to the character of an independent nation seems to have been distinguished by some token of providential agency; and in the important revolution just accomplished

in the system of their united government the tranquil deliberations and voluntary consent of so many distinct communities from which the event has resulted cannot be compared with the means by which most governments have been established without some return of pious gratitude, along with an humble anticipation of the future blessings which the past seem to presage. The reflections, arising out of the present crisis, have forced themselves too strongly on my mind to be suppressed.

And in his closing words he resorted " once more to the benign Parent of the Human Race in humble supplication that, since He has been pleased to favor the American people with opportunities for deliberating in perfect tranquillity, and dispositions for deciding with unparalleled unanimity on a form of government for the security of their union and the advancement of their happiness, so His divine blessing may be equally conspicuous in the enlarged views, the temperate consultations, and the wise measures on which the success of this Government must depend." [21]

A few days later both Houses of the new Congress replied to the President's address as was their early custom. The Senate commended the President " to the protection of Almighty God, earnestly beseeching Him long to preserve a life so valuable and dear to the people of the United States, and [hoped] that your Administration may be prosperous to the nation and glorious to yourself." [22] The House declared that "we feel with you the strongest obligations to adore the Invisible Hand which has led the American people through so many difficulties." [23] When Washington had received these responses he announced himself as "inexpressibly happy in a belief that Heaven, which has done so much for our infant nation, will not withdraw its providential influence before our political felicity shall have been completed . . . . Thus supported by a firm trust in the Great Arbiter of the Universe, aided by the collected wisdom of the Union, and imploring the divine benediction on our joint exertions in the service of our country, I readily engage with you in the arduous but pleasing task of attempting to make a nation happy." [24]

So well satisfied were the directors of the new government at the conclusion of the first session of Congress, that the two Houses united to request the President " to recommend to the people of the United States a day of public thanksgiving and prayer, to be observed by acknowledging with grateful hearts the many and signal favors of Almighty God, especially by affording them an opportunity peaceably to establish a form of government for their safety and happiness." So requested, Washington issued the first

Presidential Thanksgiving Proclamation, setting aside the fourth Thursday in November, 1789, "to be devoted . . . to the service of that great and glorious Being who is the beneficent author of all the good that was, that is, or that will be; that we may then all unite in rendering unto Him our sincere and humble thanks for His kind care and protection . . . ." Furthermore that the American people might "then unite in most humbly offering [their] prayers and supplications to the great Lord and Ruler of Nations, and beseech Him to pardon our national and other transgressions; to enable us all, whether in public or private stations, to perform our several and relative duties properly and punctually; to render our National Government a blessing to all the people by constantly being a Government of wise, just and constitutional laws . . . to promote the knowledge and practice of true religion and virtue, and the increase of science . . . and, generally, to grant unto all mankind such a degree of temporal prosperity as He alone knows to be best." [25] Likewise in his first annual message to Congress Washington set a fashion ever since followed, of referring with gratitude to a higher power directing American destiny, mentioning "the blessings which a gracious Providence has placed within our reach." [26]

Thus the new government was conceived and established by men of virtue and frugality acknowledging their indebtedness to a power greater than themselves. While their phrases were not those of the seventeenth century divines, and while gone was the doom-filled utterance of Calvinism, it was true piety albeit of a deistic restraint tinctured by the new life of reason.

But these were not the only religious influences contributing to American political ordering. While the English enterprise had been developing along the North Atlantic coast, another nation was directing a similar effort in a region eventually to be within the confines of the United States. Spain, in fact, had shown England the way, and settlements of a different nature had been established in Florida and New Mexico before Englishmen began to shake with fever on the James River.

Catholic Spain, first of all the western powers, had turned toward the New World. An adventurer sailing under her flag had discovered it and her enterprising citizens had first undertaken to plant western civilization in the Americas. Settlement had begun in 1493 and in this planting of outposts the religious motive had played a great, though different, part from similar influence in the English colonies.

The relationship between church and state in Spain had been unusually close. This was in large part due to the fact that the Moors had partially conquered the Hispanic peninsula in the first Christian millenium, and it had taken several hundred years of warfare to drive them out. These centuries had seen a series of crusades in which church and state had joined forces, and the ultimate triumph had come in 1492, the year of Columbus' great discovery.

At this psychological moment Spain was mobilized and impoverished. Its military leaders were in need of new fields of action. The Roman Catholic church, inspired by successful campaigns against the infidel, was in militant missionary frame of mind and at the same time intimately concerned with political administration. Also, the desire for wealth and power was kept bright by the light of this great success. It was but natural that wealth and power should be sought in the Indies, and as there were great hordes of savages there, the saving of countless souls was an inspiration.

The Church was active from the start. Columbus had gained the ear of Queen Isabella, in part at least through Father Juan Perez, her former confessor. His great expedition of 1493 was jointly organized by him and Juan de Fonseca, Archbishop of Seville. Columbus thought of himself as a chosen messenger of God. " God made me the messenger of the new heaven and the new earth of which He spoke in the Apocalypse of St. John . . . and He showed me where to find it." [27] At a later date Oviedo summed up the missionary accomplishment. " In lands so remote

42

from Europe . . . [the devil] has been driven out by the Christians, and our holy Catholic faith and the Church of God established."

The Church, in fact, played a vital part in creating the Spanish empire. As administrators and explorers as well as missionaries, the priests were active in all phases of the conquest. We can concern ourselves here with only one chapter of its extensive history, that of organizing community life on the far frontier.

In the course of the crusades against the Moors the Spaniards had developed a technique which with modifications they could use in America. As the Spanish wrested areas from their Moorish opponents, they selected a municipality where they established a garrison and a missionary community, to keep order and to restore the faith. The municipal center would also be a general administrative and defense headquarters. This plan was used in America. From two headquarters areas, Santo Domingo in the West Indies and then Mexico City on the mainland, a series of outposts was established intermittently for more than two centuries. When these were set up in Florida, New Mexico, Texas, Arizona, and California, they had reached the sometime boundaries of the United States.

In these five regions Spain was to create communities of a unique character. In all of them were large numbers of aboriginal inhabitants in various stages of civilization, varying from settled agricultural tribes to nomadic plainsmen. Spain was anxious to civilize and Christianize them, not only that their souls might be saved but also that the fruits of their labor might be used. Furthermore, they wished to create defense outposts against first the French and English and finally the Russians. Colonial religious activity was further vitalized by the Catholic Reformation at its height in the mid-sixteenth century and the founding of new religious orders, particularly the militant, missionary-minded Jesuits. They, together with the Dominicans and Franciscans, were to strive effectively in America.

The enterprise really began when French Huguenots sought to set up a Protestant refuge on the St. Johns River in Florida. The result was a Spanish frontier municipality located at St. Augustine in 1565. This was followed by a mission station among the Apalachee Indians in West Florida, and a fortification at Pensacola to resist the French.

The action in the New Mexico region was more of a colonizing venture. Here the natives were agricultural; some of them settled in pueblo type communal dwellings. In this region there were likewise trading possibilities. As early as 1581 efforts began. Father Juan de Oñate promoted a missionary enterprise in 1598 and by 1610 the municipality of Santa Fé was established.

The French advance into Louisiana roused Spanish

interest in Texas. Some trading activity had spread out from Santa Fé into western Texas, yet when Father Hidalgo had desired to advance into East Texas he had but slight success and so little support from the crown that he had to retreat and leave the scene of his labors. It was not until the French became firmly settled in New Orleans and in the Mississippi Valley that San Antonio was established in 1718 and the real work of organizing Texas as part of the Spanish Empire could begin.

The final move was toward the Pacific. The Spaniards' advance in northern Mexico had made them acquainted with the dreary region of Lower California, and adventurous priests like Father Kino and Father Salvatierra had penetrated into Arizona, but knowledge of California proper was still very sketchy. Then a change in Spain's fortunes, due to the general wars of the eighteenth century, England's victories and Russia's advances southward from Alaska, roused Spain's pride and apprehension; and finally the Cross and the Sword were carried into California. Don Gaspar de Portolá and Fray Junipero Serra began establishing missions and presidios along El Camino Real from San Diego to San Francisco. By 1782, just as the thirteen colonies were winning their independence, the geographical limits of the Spanish Empire were finally being marked.

This Spanish method of colonization had made

its unique contribution to the American art of self-government. Spanish empire-building particularly on these northern frontiers, had followed in some measure the religious crusade pattern of the Moorish reconquest. The plan meant creating strategic armed advanced posts in successive areas. In America this involved not the rule of rescued Spaniards but the control and civilization of aboriginal inhabitants. The most effective civilizing agency which the Spaniards used was the Church now revived in zeal by the Catholic Counter Reformation. They established forts or presidios here and there with mobile garrisons, but more important, they established mission stations, modeled on pueblos, where priests of the various orders—Franciscan, Dominican, Jesuit, or others—formed communities of Indians who were taught Christianity, some literacy, and the settled customs of agriculture, industry, and family life. In a number of these missions there was also political schooling. The Spanish authority believed in certain limited forms of local self-government on the municipal pattern. They found it psychologically effective to give certain of the Indians titles and municipal responsibilities, often on a token scale carefully supervised by the priests. Likewise they were given some military organization as local militia, with military titles and badges. As Bolton says:

It was not self-government any more than is student government in a primary school. But it was a means of control, and was a step toward self-government. It is one of the things, moreover, which helps to explain how one or two missionaries and three or four soldiers could make an orderly town out of two or three thousand barbarians recently assembled from divers and sometimes mutually hostile tribes. So deeply was it impressed upon the Indians of New Mexico that some of them yet maintain their Spanish pueblo organization, and by it still govern themselves. And, I am told, in some places even in California the descendants of the mission Indians still keep up the pueblo organization as a sort of fraternity or secret society.[28]

There were scores of these stations, some managing as many as two thousand Indians. At the height of the system, in California alone twenty-one mission stations were populated by thirty-one thousand Indians. A system as widespread as this meant that no insignificant proportion of the community life of Florida, Texas, New Mexico, and California had a base as religious as that of the English colonies, and though the contribution to democracy as presently defined was certainly not as great, nevertheless an embryo sense of self-government was there, which would develop in later comers from the east and north.

By 1790, then, the peculiarly intimate though paradoxical connection between religions and democracy had become apparent, and it has been possible to present it in evolutionary outline. A millenium of intimate relationship between church and state had produced a fusion of interest which colonial conditions and revolution itself were to alter rather than destroy. In the sixteenth and seventeenth centuries there had come the complex moves known as the Protestant Reformation and the Catholic Counter-Reformation in Western Europe and the Puritan Revolution in England. About the same time occured the discovery and settlement of America. The new world soon became a place where dreams could be realized, where discontents could be remedied, and where man's ingenuity might raise his potential for human happiness.

America seemed to be the answer to many who felt frustrated in their religious aspirations. They could not conform to the state church in England. Could they not create their own church in a new society? These men and women by-and-large were not seeking separation of church and state; rather they wished a new political-ecclesiastical organization. They came to America to create new bodies politic in the form of theocracies in which the ecclesiastical authority should be predominant. Their enterprise created self-governing communities. The traumatic experience of the wilderness provided for them a larger measure of democracy than planned and in the end produced religious liberty and the virtual separation of church and state. But despite this loosening of age-old official ties, the influence of religion was to prove stronger, probably, than if the ancient relationship of church and state had persisted. When a people, the pattern of whose thought and action was so moralistic and pietistic and so dominated by denomination and creed, created self-government, they were bound to impose upon the pattern of this government the spirit if not the form of their religion. The peculiar circumstances of the migration and settlement together with the character of so many of these citizens of Zion decreed that this religious influence should be democratic, perhaps in spite of itself.

The Religion of American Democracy

RELIGION was destined to do more than mold the institutional forms of American Democracy. It was so to infuse the polity with its spirit that in time democracy itself was to resemble a religion. The republic came into being at a singular point in history and in a place where there was a remarkable convergence of influences which were ordained, as it were, to bring about this unusual cultural phenomenon. To the mystical it might seem that this occurred because the epoch was indeed *kairos*, the fullness of time, one in which a unique combination of cultural determinants appeared, designed to produce this result.

The new United States was to be the field of action of a series of forces producing changes in the physical, intellectual, and emotional climate conditioning American institutional patterns. Body, mind, and spirit in this young nation were stimulated to that great effort which was to establish faith in men's capacity to overcome, to survive, and to construct. The most obvious influence was the existence of the great expanse of land from the Atlantic to the Mississippi, inhabited by a fringe of population in the eastern area. Prior to the completion of independence relatively few had crossed the mountains to raise new landmarks, but the ink was hardly dry on the Constitution and the Northwest Ordinance before an increasing stream began to penetrate the Dark and Bloody Ground and the Watauga Region and to establish communities in the Ohio Valley. Settlers migrated likewise into the borderlands of northern New England, and within little more than a decade four new states—Vermont, Kentucky, Tennessee, and Ohio—had been added to the galaxy of the original thirteen.

Scarcely had the young commonwealths been constructed in rudimentary fashion on distant frontiers than another impulse for expansion seized the governors of the republic. In 1803 they acquired Louisiana beyond the Mississippi and doubled the already vast area of the United States. The land which they purchased, save at New Orleans, St. Louis, and at scattered riverside outposts, was as innocent of white inhabitants as had been the Atlantic Coast. Here was the challenge of almost unlimited opportunity. Seldom was there spread before any society a greater invitation to enterprise and to new creation. The region was so vast and so stocked with potential wealth that there was no bar to anyone who had imagination, ingenuity, and fortitude enough to leave the familiar and venture into the unknown, or at least into the less well known, to mobilize wealth and create new communities. Nor was it too long after this acquisition that Florida, Texas, Oregon, and California were added. A transcontinental, truly imperial domain, had become proving ground for the vitality and capacity for social expansion and organization of this federal republic. Nothing like it existed anywhere except perhaps in the British Empire. The result was constant movement, new feats of enterprise, and an unparalleled expenditure of creative energy.

Side by side with this physical opportunity came intellectual stimulus. The Age of Reason, which could cite the United States as one of its great achievements, was giving way to a new era. The two Revolutions, American and French, had been upsetting the equilibrium of the eighteenth century. The classical age had run its course; its intellectual energy and its appeal were both spent. Hence the pendulum was bound to swing back—a contrasting romantic age was coming into being. This was an international development, spanning the Atlantic, pervading western civilization.

In the new republic, circumstances conspired to accelerate the approaching romantic age, to cause that excited stirring of the imagination which is the essence of the romantic. The cessation of the prolonged wars which had plagued the world for the century pre-

ceding the final defeat of Napoleon freed the United
States to follow the natural course of evolution which
the environment seemed to prescribe. What had not
destiny in store for this people? They had built a
series of communities. They had defended their
boundaries against alien and aboriginal foes. They
had resisted tyranny. They had humbled a great
power. They had won independence. They had
created an ingenious and workable, though complex,
system of self-government. They had played a part
in world politics which enabled themselves at least
to think of their state as a world power. They had
created a nation. Now they were undertaking to
create a culture.

Despite their distance from the centers of advanced
civilization, situated as they were, far from examples
to inspire them, they would create literature and art,
in true romantic fashion, out of the beauties and the
crudities of the wilderness; they would patronize
science and build educational institutions. All this
they would do with a sense of mission. The hopes
and prayers of the founders had been realized. Man
had created a new estate where each could realize his
potential to the utmost. Mankind had reached new
stature in the new world. In the spirit of liberty and
equality, with unlimited opportunity available to all,
the ideal community dreamed of by religious zealots
of the Reformation or intellectual rationalists of the

Enlightenment had been achieved. It was now the duty of the republic to proclaim its achievement to the world in the true spirit of romanticism.

But in addition to this physical and intellectual change in climate there was another to which much less consideration has been given. There was a change in the spiritual climate as well. There came a new interest in and yearning for individual salvation from sin. There were many and complex circumstances attendant upon and contributing to this manifestation. The basic fact is that a large proportion of those who set the patterns of American folkways were people who by a process of natural selection were whole-heartedly committed to Calvinism. Following the preaching of the stern Genevan, made no whit easier by the dour Scots divines, their disciples bowed in awe before the omnipotent, omniscient, and omnipresent Jehovah who had created man, by nature totally depraved and sinful, and then had provided for His creatures a rigorous process whereby a chosen group could achieve salvation from their sin and dwell with Him forever. Those who were to be thus saved had been predestined for this end from the beginning of time. However, the plan of salvation involved defeat as well as victory. Certain of the depraved creatures were not to overcome their depravity, would be defeated, and must therefore suffer the punishment of eternal damnation. These, too, had been predestined for this awful fate from the beginning. This was the contrasting system of victory and defeat which had been established to give certain men the opportunity to win salvation.

The great question in the minds of many, convinced as they were that their fate had been predestined, was to find out what this fate was. This they could discover only by a life of intense self-examination, by an even morbid absorption in their own thoughts and conduct. In this way the individual sought to discover signs of grace in an ability to fight and conquer sin. Many, therefore, became extreme activists. For, if through action of grace these signs were discoverable, men might believe they were of the elect; but if such signs were absent, then would the gates of Hell seem to be yawning. As the rigors of early American existence had given way to more settled and comfortable life, and as signs of independence, democratic opportunity, and success became more universal, this concept of social stratification—in which one group was destined to be an aristocratic elite of the saved and another to be hopeless failures, eternally damned—grew to seem more incongruous and contrary to the facts of democratic society.

The alternative religious concept hitherto available had been the pale rationalism of deism which acknowledged the existence of a Creator and Lawgiver.

He had made a great machine and set it running according to a fixed and immutable pattern. Thereafter the Creator ceased to have any concern with the affairs of men. Such a rational concept was cold and could have little appeal save to the coldly rational. It gave little comfort to the suffering or sorrowing, little strength to those who were discouraged or lacking in confidence, little courage to those who were timid and fearful. After a half century or so it failed to satisfy and interest in it eventually almost disappeared. After the Revolution the listlessness of deism palled. There was increasing yearning for stimulating, emotional, religious experience, more invigorating than deism and less pessimistic than Calvinism.

Even before the American Revolution there were evidences of a revolt against the cold formality of Calvinism with its morbid introspection: signs of a new spirit appeared in the Great Awakening. After the winning of independence had been accomplished, in the bustle and enthusiasm of the creation of a new republic with many interior communities, new optimism began to blossom; a new sense of opportunity began to bloom. Also new churches were in the making. The Baptists were spreading out their congregations. Wesley and Whitefield had been followed by Asbury, and Methodism was taking form. The doctrines of Calvin were giving way to those of the Dutch theologian, Arminius, who had declared for freedom of choice, and maintained both that grace abounded for all and that salvation was free. Man was not predestined to one state or the other; he was free to accept or to reject. Almost simultaneously with the realization of political independence, Americans began to awaken to a new sense of freedom of personal destiny. Quite in the spirit of the adventurous future offered by the frontier, and of the freedom of the imagination born of the new romanticism, came a great wave of religious enthusiasm based upon a new sense of the possibility of salvation from sin and freedom from the aristocratic strictures of Calvinism. From the early 1790's until the late 1850's, rolled in a cumulative wave of religious experience of tremendous import.

A sporadic series of religious revivals appeared in all parts of the new republic at some time or other during these years. In the colleges, in country churches, in tumultuous camp meetings, and in city parishes, all Protestant denominations shared in these outpourings. At the turn of the century there were an Awakening on the frontier and revivals in New England. Right after the War of 1812 there was a series of protracted meetings in New England; Asahel Nettleton and President Timothy Dwight of Yale were the leaders. Daniel Baker wrought mightily in the South, and Charles G. Finney preached in New

York State and over in Ohio. These enthusiasms were pronounced in every decade, particularly in the 1800's, 1820's, 1830's, and in the grand climax of 1858.

These preachers brought a new outlook on life, a new interpretation of the meaning of existence. Under orthodox Calvinism the individual was helpless; he was predestined either to be saved or damned. God had ordered his state from the beginning of time and he must obediently occupy the station to which it had pleased God to call him, for it was all for God's greater glory. But the appeal of the revivalist often was not in the static, helpless terms of Calvinism but in the exalting terms of the contrasting Arminian doctrine. Salvation was not reserved for the elect; salvation was free. Any who repented their sins, threw themselves on God's mercy, and accepted Jesus Christ as their personal Savior, for them grace would abound; the chains of their sins would be loosed; the fear of Hell erased; and sanctified in their faith they would stand redeemed, purified, washed in the blood of the Lamb slain to redeem the world. This was a blessed freedom; it was available to all and it would continue for all eternity when the saved would dwell with relatives and friends. This crashing democracy of salvation was a tremendous revolution. As in Adam all men shall die, so in Christ shall all be made alive—and the word was *all*. What a stupendous decree of liberty!

So to countless numbers came regeneration, the release from the weight of sin, the fear of Hell. Conscience was composed. Ineffable happiness was the accompaniment of the renewal of faith, that faith which could remove mountains. No longer was church membership formal and attendance at worship a duty. One went to God's house to rejoice with the brotherhood of the redeemed; *there* flowed the water of life, constantly refreshing.

The fact that salvation came to so many had a tremendous effect upon the life of the nation. It is my purpose to attempt an outline of it, for we have neglected in our writing of American history to give due consideration to the nature and consequences of this widespread and really tremendous experience which influenced and altered the lives of such a multitude. This period of recurring, almost constant, religious revival produced, in effect, what can be likened to another revolution, an Arminian Revolution. This emotional transformation had a terrific impact upon American society and upon the young democracy. It produced an equality such as no Declaration or Constitution, no statute, no law or decree could ever prescribe.

In the course of this great revolution a series of social factors and behavior patterns conditioned by them emerged in a fashion which deserves the closest attention. Examining available statistics we perceive fairly accurately what the situation was. Of the thirty-one million people in the United States in 1860 we can find ground to believe that five million professed some form of membership in Christian churches. Of these approximately four-fifths were Protestants and one-fifth Catholics. Making a rough projection of church membership against the total population one could venture to say that of the thirty-one million people something like twenty-five million would think of themselves as Protestants as contrasted to any other form of religious designation. In other words there were about 80 per cent who from a cultural standpoint would manifest Protestant behavior characteristics. These were divided roughly into more than forty sects. Of these numbers over half were Methodists and Baptists, with the Presbyterians the only near competitors. These three groups made up 75 per cent of the Protestants.

As de Tocqueville discovered more than a century ago, and as a recent scholar has once again pointed out, these numerous Christians " created a new pattern of church-state relations, unknown since the first century. It was called the ' voluntary system ' to distinguish it from the state-church tradition in Europe." [1] This relationship came into complete realization when the last tax support for churches was abolished in Connecticut in 1818 and in Massachusetts in 1833. This voluntary system meant that, though official connection between church and state had ceased, religion was so consuming an interest of such a large section of the population that its influence was manifest everywhere. There were more than thirty-eight thousand church buildings and on many horizons the church spire pointing heavenward was the dominating landmark. These pious reminders rose over the cities and their bells periodically called all who would to worship. In town and village, they were frequently the most imposing structures, whose only rival might be the courthouse. In most of these thousands of churches were clergymen constantly preaching the Word of God or through liturgical observance leading the communities in worship. The church and its leadership occupied central places in the life of most societies and even the indifferent or the antagonistic could not escape consciousness of them.

Other evidences of this voluntary but close relationship of church and society are endless. The whole system of the administration of justice was based upon oaths and the belief in a system of future rewards and punishments. Oaths were administered in the name of God and taken on the Bible. Most legislative bodies had chaplains, and their law-making was initiated daily with prayer. Most officials, executive, legislative and judicial, were required to take oaths of office on entering their duties. Frequently there were laws requiring respect of the Sabbath and laws against blasphemy. In times of crisis, public days of prayer and fasting were proclaimed. Annually there were days of public thanksgiving. Most community ceremonies were opened with prayer. Though the schools were public and non-sectarian there was daily Bible-reading in many of them. In certain of the New England states a clergyman preached an annual election sermon to the legislature before it proceeded to elect the state officers.

In the lives of many of those who attended church there was rather strenuous and constant religious exercise. The frequent revival services, the strength of feeling involved in conversion, the need for public profession and, in some denominations, periods of probation, were moving and exalting experiences; while the final witness in certain of the churches was immersion in water, oftentimes in some icy stream or pond. Then came the orderly sequence of observance. On Sunday there were two services and Sunday School, and during the week there were frequently two evening meetings for prayer and testimony. In some of the denominations those who had been lax were required to appear for public examination to be absolved or condemned, to repent and to seek forgiveness. These were strenuous and life-filling experiences, and frequently they brought such rewards as only those who have sought salvation from sin and have achieved it can understand. But testimony reveals that such a sense of salvation is the true state of liberty, and when the Arminian Revolution made this liberty available to all, it established the true equality of men, for all were children of God, alike in His sight, joint heirs with Christ. Christian liberty was to many the great exemplification or instrument of democracy.

Another characteristic of the life of the nineteenth century which stimulated religious interest and made it so intense was the prevalence of bad health and the uncertain life expectancy. In this era there was a series of epidemics such as yellow fever and cholera. There was much malaria. A people who had been working with their muscles out-of-doors were being confined in ill-ventilated factories, shops, and offices. Their muscles were growing flabby, while their huge intake of heavy food continued. Their oxygen supply was cut down, for since they no longer worked in the outdoors, they got less air during the day, and as there was a prevailing belief that night air was bad, they got none during the dark watches. The results were dyspepsia and tuberculosis. Finally, the birth rate was high and infant mortality distressing. All this added up to the constant presence of the Angel of Death, frequent bereavement, and periodic emotional disturbance through grief, fear, and sympathy. If, as was often the case, there might well be an average of one death every three years in each household, there was a constant need for neighborly ministration. When death struck, it was the neighborly thing to do to help, to comfort, and in a real sense to share grief.

Religion was mightily affected by this situation. Bereavement was the will of God. Those who were taken were released from the cares and pains of earth to the happiness of Heaven. Many, particularly the children, were early to enter realms of bliss and, escaping the perils of life, were to dwell for eternity with God. In Heaven they would be seen again. The separation was but for a little while; then there would be the joyful reunion on the other shore. Clergymen and friends alike hastened to offer this comfort; weeping would be only for a season, and then the joy of meeting to part no more. The constant recurrence of this experience produced a Christian relationship in the communities and particularly in the churches, a fellowship of suffering, which brought neighbors into close association and strengthened the religious tie. In communities where death was so frequent, religion had much consolation and was an essential part of that which made existence bearable.

The nature of the dominants of behavior shaped by this religious interpretation of existence is seen most vividly in the type of education which was generally offered to the children. This education was so effectively to impress upon succeeding generations an outlook on life and a way of living that it was perhaps the most potent force molding the American Way, and it was so formulated that it in effect made democracy not only a government but a way of life. This pattern began in earliest childhood and can be best understood by some quotations from books which were widely read by children of the most numerous Protestant groups. The self-identification taught a child was based on a personal relationship with God. Isaac Watts wrote many verses, and in a little book for children called *Watt's Songs Divine and Moral for the Use of Children,* he wrote a hymn called " Solemn Thoughts on God and Death," which very carefully explained to the child the nature of this relationship:

> There is a God, that reigns above,
>> Lord of the heavens, and earth, and seas:
> I fear His wrath, I ask His love,
>> And with my lips I sing His praise.
>
> There is a law which He has writ,
>> To teach us all what we must do;
> My soul, to His commands submit,
>> For they are holy, just and true.
>
> There is a gospel of rich grace,
>> Whence sinners all their comforts draw;

Lord, I repent, and seek Thy face,
  For I have often broke Thy law.

There is an hour when I must die,
  Nor do I know how soon 'twill come;
A thousand children, young as I,
  Are called by death to hear their doom.

Let me improve the hours I have,
  Before the day of grace has fled;
There's no repentance in the grave,
  Nor pardon offered to the dead.

Just as a tree cut down, that fell
  To north or southward, there it lies;
So man departs to heaven or hell,
  Fixed in the state wherein he dies.[2]

This concept of existence was emphasized in story books with large print and pictures, which taught simple lessons about the children's relationship to God. One of them by " Aunt Susan," entitled *Little Susy's Little Servants*, impressed upon little girls the obligation to dedicate their hands, feet, ears, eyes, and tongue to the service of their Heavenly Father. Susy's father was able to explain this obligation to his daughter so effectively that she vowed then and there:

"Yes, papa, I will."

Then they knelt down together and Susy's papa prayed to God to hear all they had been saying, and to be so good as to accept all Susy had now promised to give Him, and to keep her from ever forgetting her promise, but to make it her rule in all she said and all she did, all she saw and all she heard, to remember,

" I am not my own." [3]

In this way God's presence became very real very early in life, as indicated in another little volume published by the American Tract Society, entitled *The Deserter*, wherein a little child is described as saying:

But I could not hide myself from a sense of God's presence, His eye seemed everywhere, diving into the very depths of my heart. It started a train of influences which, God be praised, I never ceased to feel. If I was ever tempted to any secret sin, ' Thou God Seest Me,' stared me in the face, and I stood back restrained and awed. [4]

This concept of the imminence of God and the consequent desirability of obedience was further emphasized in terms of death, which in those days was so frequent an occurrence. The authors of these books for children frequently impressed upon them the uncertainty of life as in another publication of the American Tract Society which appeared in two small volumes, one for boys and the other for girls, both entitled *Helps Over Hard Places*, written by

Lynde Palmer. In that designed for little girls they were cautioned in terms which could not fail to be impressive:

> Press on, dear little ones. Do not turn aside into the pleasant bypaths, no matter how rough the way may be. And if at last, in the twilight, you come into a strange, dim land, and begin to tremble a little at the shadows, you shall hear a sweet voice say,—"Fear not, little flock, for it is your Father's good pleasure to give you the kingdom."
>
> And if, still later, you come to a dark, cold river, and the worn little feet falter, and can not go any further, then will the Good Shepherd come, and tenderly lifting all the tired lambs, he will carry them safe in his bosom.[5]

The idea was expressed even more emphatically in *The A. B. C. Picture Book:*

> I have got a great many stories to tell you; but I will not tell them now. One of these days, if we all live, I will tell you more stories.
>
> I said, "If *we all live.*" Children, as well as grown-up people, may die. My dear child, you may die before I make another book for you. I hope you will not die so soon; but you may. Be good children, then. Learn to love Jesus Christ, and try to do as he tells little children

to do in the Bible. Think how the Saviour died
for you. Do you not think that you ought to love
him? Try to be like him. Pray that you may be
like him; that you may have a new heart; that
you may be kept from sin; that you may be fit to
go to heaven when you die. If you are good,
then you will be happy if you die while you are
little; and you will be happy if you live to grow
up. But I cannot say any more now. Good bye! [6]

While the author of " My Country 'Tis of Thee,"
the Rev. S. F. Smith, put it in verse form in a small
book, *Lyric Gems*:

> Go to thy rest, my child,
>   Go to thy dreamless bed,
> Gentle and undefiled,
>   With blessings on thy head.
>
> Fresh roses in thy hand,
>   Buds on thy pillow laid;
> Haste from this fearful land,
>   Where flowers so quickly fade.
>
> Before thy heart had learned
>   In waywardness to stray;
> Before thy feet had turned
>   The dark and downward way;
>
> Ere sin had seared the breast,
>   Or sorrow woke the tear;
> Rise to thy home of rest,
>   In yon celestial sphere.

Because thy smile was fair,
  Thy lip and eye so bright,
Because thy cradle-care
  Was such a fond delight,—

Shall love, with weak embrace,
  Thy heavenward wing detain?
No!—angel, seek thy place
  Amid heaven's cherub train.[7]

When these children were a little older they were
presented with books designed to offer them private
and inspirational counsel. Jacob Abbott, the author
of the famous *Rollo* books, prepared such a guide
entitled *The Young Christian*. In this he asked the
question:

> Do you never feel unquiet in spirit, restless or
> sad? Do you never experience a secret uneasi-
> ness of heart, of which you do not know the
> exact cause, but which destroys, or at least dis-
> turbs your peace? If you do, take this course.
> Instead of flying from those feelings when they
> come into your heart, *advance boldly to meet
> them.* Grasp and examine them. Find their
> cause. You will find in nine cases out of ten that
> their cause is *something wrong* in your own con-
> duct or character. Young persons will generally
> find something wrong towards their parents. Now
> go and confess these faults. Do not endeavor
> to palliate or excuse them, but endeavor on the

other hand to see their worst side, and if you confess them freely and fully, and resolve to sin no more, peace will return, at least, so far as these causes have banished it from your heart.[8]

Daniel Wise wrote in *The Young Man's Counsellor*:

Say, then, young man, which is the choice of wisdom? As a mere question of advantage during the present life, ought you not to lay a foundation of evangelical piety? I appeal to the tribunal of your reason. I demand the verdict of your intellect. To enforce that, I implore the authority of your conscience. With your reason and conscience on the side of religion, I beg you to yield a submissive will! And, hearken! A higher voice than mine supports this appeal! From Him whom " the heaven of heavens cannot contain," a sound, " still, small," but thrilling, steals into every young man's heart, saying, "WILT THOU NOT, FROM THIS TIME, CRY UNTO ME, MY FATHER, THOU ART THE GUIDE OF MY YOUTH!"

Take heed how you despise this appeal of your Creator! Look at your life, in its relations to him, and to eternity! Contemplate your destinies from that " height which no duration limits,—where Hope spreads in immensity her indefatigable wings,—where you can feel within yourself a secret force, which bears you above all time, as a light body rises from the depth of the sea. From this height, look into this narrow valley, where the first term of your existence is to be accomplished." And thus, with both worlds before you, come to the great decision to lay your foundation surely and steadfastly on Him who is the "Rock of ages."

To be successful in life, to rise above the common herd of mankind, a young man requires certain elements of character;—all of which are attainable through the power of religion, and many of which most young men never will attain without that power. He must possess IN-TEGRITY, that he may win public confidence; INTELLIGENCE, that he may command respect; INDUSTRY, that he may collect honey from the flowers of trade; ECONOMY and frugality, to preserve his gains; ENERGY, by which to surmount obstacles; and TACT, to enable him to adapt himself to the openings of Providence, and to make him the man for the hour of opportunity. These qualifications are, to success in life, as foundations of jasper to a royal palace. Whoever possesses them cannot be an inferior man. To that man who retains them, life cannot be a failure. Nay, he must rise to social superiority; he must win a commanding influence. And, hear me, young man! These elements of success are all attainable, in a greater or less degree, by every youth who will cordially embrace, and faithfully adhere to, the religion of Christ; as I will endeavor to prove, in the succeeding chapters.[9]

A solicitous clergyman, Rev. Dr. David Magie, in his *Spring-Time of Life*, gave his sincerest counsel in moving words:

> I look forward a few years, and find children become youth, and youth men and women in active life. The seeds sown in infancy by some fond mother have swelled and grown, and become trees of righteousness, and the lessons given by a kind father are yielding their appropriate fruit. One comes out and joins himself to the industrious, the prudent and the pious; while another associates with the indolent, the dissipated and the profane. From this point you may trace their destiny for two worlds. Let me see how youth assort themselves in the school, the workshop and the college, and I need no prophet's ken to predict what they will be and what they will do when they become men. Viciously inclined as a young man may be, a virtuous companionship is often the means of his salvation. Virtuously disposed as he may be, an unhappy association may work his ruin.
>
> Reflect, then, my young friend, seriously and prayerfully, on the importance of the season through which you are now passing. Little do you think how deep an interest is felt for your

welfare. There is the man that begat you, and the woman that bare you, each crying out, "My son, if thy heart shall be wise, my heart shall rejoice, even mine." Kind friends draw near and ask for blessings on your heads, which shall reach to the utmost bounds of the everlasting hills. Your minister prays that you may become his joy and the crown of his rejoicing in the day of the Lord Jesus. Above all, God himself looks down, and blending His claims with your highest welfare, speaks out, "My son, give me thy heart." Oh, shall all this interest be felt for you, in heaven and on earth, in vain! Will you not at this early hour on the dial of human life, realize the grandeur and glory of the destiny that awaits you!

Be faithful to yourselves, to your fellow men, and to God for ten, fifteen, or twenty years, and I almost dare promise you a useful life, a happy death, and a blissful immortality.[10]

Even more effective in continuing these lessons and firmly fixing this interpretation of the meaning and nature of existence were the school books. One of the most widely used was a prose work of the great Dr. Isaac Watts on *Improvement of the Mind*, which might be called psychology. He laid down a series of rules of which two are quoted:

I. Rule

Deeply possess your mind with the vast importance of a good judgment, and the rich and inestimable advantage of right reasoning. Review the instances of your own misconduct in life; think seriously with yourselves how many follies and sorrows you had escaped, and how much guilt and misery you had prevented, if from your early years you had but taken due pains to judge aright concerning persons, times, and things. This will awaken you with lively vigour to address yourselves to the work of improving your reasoning powers, and of seizing every opportunity and advantage for that end.

II. Rule

Consider the weaknesses, frailties, and mistakes of human nature in general, which arise from the very constitution of a soul united to an animal body, and subjected to many inconveniences thereby. Consider the many additional weaknesses, mistakes, and frailties, which are derived from our original apostacy and fall from a state of innocence; how much our powers of understanding are yet more darkened, enfeebled, and imposed on by our senses, our fancies, and our unruly passions, &c. Consider the depth and difficulty of many truths and the flattering appearance of falsehood, whence arise an infinite number of dangers to which we are exposed in our judgment of things. Read with greediness those authors who treat of the doctrine of prejudices, prepossessions, and springs of error, on purpose to make your soul watchful on all sides, that it suffer not itself as far as possible to be imposed on by any of them.[11]

Such purpose is also evident in the early type of *English Reader*, such as that written by Lindley Murray:

Diligence, industry, and proper improvement of time, are material duties of the young.

The acquisition of knowledge is one of the most honourable occupations of youth.

Whatever useful or engaging endowments we possess, virtue is requisite, in order to their shining with proper lustre.

Virtuous youth gradually brings forward accomplished and flourishing manhood.

Sincerity and truth form the basis of every virtue.

Disappointments and distress are often blessings in disguise . . . .

Our ignorance of what is to come, and of what is really good or evil, should correct anxiety about worldly success.

The veil which covers from our sight the events of succeeding years, is a veil woven by the hand of mercy.

The best preparation for all the uncertainties

of futurity, consists in a well ordered mind, a good conscience, and a cheerful submission to the will of Heaven.[12]

Science was designed to teach the same outlook in a small book by Mrs. Phelps called *Natural Philosophy*:

> Let the young continue to follow this early impulse of the mind to seek knowledge. In the study of Natural Philosophy, there are important advantages. It leads to useful inventions; to the habit of observing and reasoning; it elevates and enlarges the mind, and gives the soul new and delightful views of the power and goodness of God.[13]

In these days early in the child's education he might be given a book on *Natural Theology* by Rev. T. H. Gallaudet:

> Natural Theology is not learned from the Bible. It is all that can be known about God, merely by examining the beings and things which he has made, without the aid of revealed Theology.
>
> The beings and things which God has made, and causes to be, or live and grow, are called *natural*, to distinguish them from the things that men make.
>
> The things that men make, are called, *works*

of art; but all that God has made, we call, the *works of nature*. By examining and studying the works of nature, we can see that there must be a God, who made and preserves all things and beings; and we can learn many things about him, which will show us his great power and wisdom, and goodness.

All the knowledge which we can thus gain, about God, is called Natural Theology; and it is this knowledge, my young friends, which I wish, in some degree, to give you, in this book that I have written for you. I hope you will be so much interested in gaining this knowledge, that you will seek for more of it, as you grow older, in larger books which have been written on the same subject, but which it might, now, be difficult for you to understand.[14]

The child's concept of democracy itself was delineated in *Peter Parley's Common School History* by Samuel G. Goodrich:

What a glorious prospect for our country, if our present government continues, if the people are true to their own interests, and maintain the liberty their fathers left them!

I say, if the people are true to their own interest. We live in a fine country, we have a good form of government, but these will not insure happiness. If the people become indolent, or if they become wicked, ruin and desolation will visit this land. Government may be compared to a house; those who live in it must take good care of it.

They must keep their doors and windows shut, to prevent storms from driving in. If any part decays, or is injured by a tempest, it must be repaired. The fires must be watched at night. In short, the whole establishment must be taken care of by people who are worthy of being trusted, people who are skilful, and who cannot be tempted to neglect their duty.

If the house is intrusted to careless, ignorant, or faithless people, it may take fire, and the inhabitants be burned up. Or it may decay and fall down upon the heads of those who dwell in it. Or it may become leaky, so as to admit the cold wind, or the driving rain or snow. It may thus become a miserable and comfortless habitation.

It is so with government. If careless, ignorant, or faithless rulers are chosen to take care of the country, wars and commotions may follow; poverty and vice may spread over the land; ignorance and misery may take the place of knowledge and prosperity. Thus the government, which, like a house, is designed to protect us, when ill managed, like a house on fire, or borne down by the tempest, may be the cause of our ruin.

Think of these things, my young readers, and when you become men, always use your influence to have no other rulers than those who are capable, honest, and sincere friends of the country.[15]

The whole philosophy was succinctly summed up in *The Lady's Almanac*:

Our summing-up must be short. The heart of our country lives in its homes, and after all the eloquent things we say about republican rights, the final test of institutions is in the domestic character of the people. The world is an enjoyable place just so far as we can render it tributary to our homes; and freedom is a blessing exactly up to the measure that we improve its privileges in forming ourselves after the divine ideal of noble men and women. Side by side stand the Altar of Liberty and the Altar of Home; and if Christianity has lighted their flames, let us never forget that it is from those flames, burning heavenward with steady strength of warmth and lustre, that Providence brings the fiery swords which arm us for our highest achievements and our grandest victories.[16]

The cumulative effect of the widespread indoctrination of children with this Christian ethic generated during the Arminian Revolution was to create an intense moral imperative which was similar to that motivating many of the migrating founders of the

republic. This morality, firmly fixed by early education, created an interpretation of the nation's mission
and destiny which was to be strengthened constantly,
and ever more widely disseminated, by the statements
of political leaders and publicists. Such men over the
years formulated a series of striking statements em-
bodying this Christian concept, in effect creating a
wisdom literature, or scripture, which cumulatively
became a directing portion of popular thinking and of
national self-definition. The precepts in turn have
played a large part in determining our behavior, our
way of life.

This new and most dynamic expression of American purpose was reflected in the propaganda for a
series of moral enthusiasms for governmental action
which came to flowering in the 1830's, when the
Arminian Revolution was at its height. In these
years the moral imperative was stimulating a concern
about sin and a yearning for perfection which pro-
foundly influenced the course of events and signifi-
cantly shaped the new American democracy of the
Age of Jackson during the Rise of the Common Man.
The growth of the population, the creation of new
communities, the development of factory production,
the extension of the right to vote, combined to create
a wider participation in the public responsibility for
government; and, therefore, the moral attitudes of
the voters had greater significance. These attitudes

were reflected in enthusiasm for reforms which were in themselves clearly related to the widely felt hatred of sin. Men of wealth moved by some of the revivalists formed a " benevolent empire." They sat on many boards of charitable directorates and backed reform with their money. There were numerous " causes " which were advocated with moral enthusiasm; three of them, the anti-bank, anti-liquor, and anti-slavery crusades, may be cited as examples.

The growth of the nation, extending new communities into the west and stimulating all sorts of venturing with capital, brought banking into the foreground and focussed attention particularly upon the Bank of the United States, chartered by the government and acting as its fiscal agent. Its power over development was great and in its exercise of that power the corporation made enemies and caused a large section of the people to become critical of its policies. In the controversy that developed and in the program which President Andrew Jackson formulated, fought for, and carried through, a definite reflection of this moral-religious concept is obvious. The Bank was evil. To the more fervent Jacksonians it was " The Great Monster " and Jackson, himself, was the prophet of righteousness battling to destroy something wicked. Such was of course not the only role which Old Hickory assumed, but it was not the least effective of his performances. The nation responded and many joined with alacrity in a crusade to suppress that which was spawned of Satan.

Simultaneously the expansion of machine industry introduced the factory system which in turn developed the factory towns with their masses of poorly paid workers crowded together in conditions often approaching squalor. In these communities the tavern became a center for convivial escape from the sordid realities of life, and the excessive use of liquor in such places served to underline and emphasize the fact that there was a too general prevalence of the social evil of intemperance. Not only in the new communities but also in rural districts this excess was obvious. Worse in the eyes of some was the fact that it was observable even in some church circles. The time had come to fight the sin of drunkenness and to develop political means to dry up the sources of liquor. So a temperance crusade against evil grew in intensity. Intemperance and drunkenness were sins, and these sins must be stamped out. Law must be invoked in the name of righteousness so that temptation might be removed by making liquor harder to obtain. In most intense form this meant the prohibition of its sale.

Most difficult of the political questions in which the moral imperative was effective was the question of human bondage. By mid-nineteenth century the institution of Negro slavery in the communities of the United States was three centuries old and thus firmly rooted. But it was not equally distributed. It had eventually proved unsuited to the economic and cultural conditions found in most sections, for it could be continued only where labor was needed for simple tasks in large gangs, namely, in tobacco, rice, sugar, and cotton planting. In regions where this type of agriculture proved convenient and profitable, the institution survived the growing sense of its inconsistency with the freedom which should be characteristic of a republic founded on the twin concepts of liberty and equality. In the South, however, it seemed that in no other way could the labor for their lush agriculture be found in the large numbers which the planters wished to employ. Besides, the care of the master for his slave made the institution a civilizing agent, a positive good. The institution was thus given an anachronistic extension of life because of a complex physiographic, economic, and cultural determinism which had fairly definite geographical-political limits; i. e., it was to be contained within fifteen regionally concentrated political units, the so-called Southern States.

This regional concentration of slavery in a growing society produced a political instrument which was much used by various elements who wished either to maintain or to secure power. Thus a conflict arose in which the moral imperative was the driving force impelling men to use this instrument. There was a general feeling throughout the world that human slavery was evil. Religiously motivated people responded to this feeling by earnestly striving to eradicate the sin, just as they wished to destroy the Monster Bank and the Demon Rum. Publicist and preacher united in tactics employed by the revivalists of the Arminian Revolution to arouse public opinion against the wickedness of owning, exploiting, and abusing human flesh and at the same time pandering to lust and sadism. Slavery must be abolished and the Southern political power based on it destroyed.

The fact of the geographic-political concentration of slavery meant that any attacks upon the institution produced a cultural conflict. The United States was in fact in a complex state of cultural development in which both a national culture and regional cultures, some older than the nation, were in parallel existence. The conflict over slavery developed into an assault of one sub-culture upon another, North upon South, and the dispute was formulated in moral-religious terms well understood in each. The South was pilloried by Northern critics as sinful and deserving of the punishments of Hell. A stern and righteous God, angry at this evil, was called upon by extremists to destroy the Southern Sodom and Gomorrah.

But within the culture under attack, the South,

there were the same moral imperatives at work. There the flame of religious enthusiasm burned just as brightly. The Arminian Revolution had swept Southern communities as well as Northern. Here was the same hatred of sin and fear of Hell, the same eagerness to serve God and enjoy the salvation made possible by the sacrificial death of Christ. The charge of sin was therefore resisted. By searching the Scriptures, Southern partisans brought forth proof that slavery was recognized and approved in both Old and New Testaments. Slavery was not a sin but a Christian institution.

Furthermore, Southern moralists maintained that these charges of sin did not come with good grace from those who worshipped the mammon of wealth, who tolerated a wage slavery which was worse than Negro slavery because it was socially irresponsible, and who were dishonestly breaking the covenant agreed upon in 1787 by trying to destroy the sacred rights of the state which they were pledged to respect. Northern abolitionists, they charged, were whited sepulchres, inwardly full of uncleanness, pious hypocrites interested only in destroying Southern political influence so as to fasten their own tyranny upon an independent, cultured, enlightened South which would be thereby degraded. The South, as a benevolent, God-fearing society, teaching heathens the Gospel of Christ and thus providing them with the means of salvation, would resist the hypocrisy of Scribes and Pharisees who sought to invite money-changers into the temple. They would not submit to accusations made by those who declared the Constitution a league with death and a covenant with Hell.

The earnestness, the dedication, the single-mindedness, and the moral intensity of religious conviction produced a conflict in which the most zealous on both sides felt themselves called of God to destroy evil and to protect themselves and their communities from sin. This religious motivation was, however, complicated, because there was an element of doubt among minorities on both sides as to the righteousness of their respective causes. In the South there were those who could not fail to realize that slavery was an anachronism and that it did give unusual opportunity for cruelty and carnal abuse. There was a resulting confusion in their consciences which actually recognized much of the strength of the charge that slavery was sinful. This inner conflict, however, was suppressed. This suppression only intensified the controversy, since the prevailing Southern mores demanded the continuance of slavery and therefore had to destroy doubt by an intensified vehemence of protestation that slavery was a divine institution ordained by God. Yet, there were many who refused to conform. Later, when war broke out, some fled to the mountains; others formed guerrilla bands which harassed the Confederates.

In the North, on the other hand, there were many who were devoted to the sacredness of law and the inviolability of contracts. The fundamental law of the Constitution protected Southerners in the possession of property rights and in their right to determine their own institutions. It was wrong to deny Southerners their due and to fight them as they sought to protect their liberties. The Northern minority dared to proclaim its beliefs at the risk of being called "Copperheads" and occasionally imprisoned. The conscience of this minority likewise confused the issue and complicated and prolonged the conflict because it denounced the Administration, hindered enlistment and, to a certain extent, gave aid and comfort to the Confederacy.

This confused and complex conflict of moralities, intensified by the emotional exaggeration of the Arminian Revolution, was not the least of the influences driving men to the shedding of blood. Those who had been freed from sin were under charge to destroy it, lest it in turn destroy others. They had no alternative and they could not compromise. This moral intensity was made most manifest by the startling witness of John Brown, who began the bloodshed in order to destroy the sin of slavery, speaking in the name of the Lord. Brown's invasion alarmed the slaveholding societies, who literally feared for their existence. They prayed to be delivered from Yankee greed and cruelty, which were sending forth men of wrath and violence to destroy that way of life which to them was sacred, a positive good.

Certain of these states proceeded, then, to take the measures which they believed necessary to protect themselves; they would secede. They followed the forms used in 1776 and, although there was no formal Declaration of Independence, South Carolina, the first state to sever the tie, issued a " Declaration of the Immediate Causes which Induce and Justify the Secession." In this recital they bore heavily upon the moral turpitude exhibited by their Northern neighbors in breaking a sacred contract, engaging in the stealing of property, and inciting slaves to insurrection. These neighbors not only had declared the leading Southern institution to be sinful, but they had justified their errors by " the sanctions of a more erroneous religious belief," i. e., the concept of a divinely ordained law " higher " than the Constitution which was their authority for the violation of this sacred compact. They likewise invoked the witness of God in the language of the original Declaration of Independence " appealing to the Supreme Judge of the World for the rectitude of our intentions." [17]

When the Southern delegates assembled at Montgomery, Alabama, in February, 1861, to create the new Confederacy, they came in the mood of reformers determined to destroy corruption and sin. The documents which they formulated sought to improve the old Constitution by eliminating opportunities for corrupting grants of money, resources, and subsidy. Likewise they took care not to repeat the error of the Founders of 1787 who ignored God. In the preamble of the Provisional Constitution they invoked the favor of Almighty God, while in the opening of the permanent Constitution they invoked not only His favor but His guidance.

The two new Presidents in their inaugural addresses gave evidence of a piety characteristic of them both. Davis's words were:

> Reverently let us invoke the God of our fathers to guide and protect us in our efforts to perpetuate the principles which by His blessing they were able to vindicate, establish and transmit to their posterity. With the continuance of His favor ever gratefully acknowledged, we may hopefully look forward to success, to peace and to prosperity.[18]

Two weeks later Lincoln proclaimed his faith that " intelligence, patriotism, Christianity and a firm reliance on Him who has never yet forsaken this favored land are still competent to adjust in the best way all our present difficulty." [19]

When the war came, each President addressed his Congress in terms expressing firm belief in the righteousness of his particular cause. Davis, again speaking first, explained the Confederacy's struggle as one for the protection of the sacred rights of social contract against a wilful and unscrupulous aggression. The South had been compelled to act to protect its liberties. "We feel that our cause is just and holy . . . . We desire peace . . . . With a firm reliance on that Divine Power which covers with its protection the just cause, we will continue to struggle for our inherent right to freedom, independence and self-government." [20] Lincoln defined the contest likewise as one to preserve the right of self-government. The government of the United States by his definition was a people's government with the responsibility of elevating the condition of men, to afford all a fair chance. The war was being fought to protect this unique experiment against a disgruntled minority who were striving to destroy it. He concluded: "And having thus chosen our course, without guile, and with pure purpose, let us renew our trust in God, and go forward without fear, and with manly hearts." [21]

In this first year of war both Presidents proclaimed days of prayer and fasting. Davis again took the lead and issued his call:

Knowing that none but a just and righteous

cause can gain the Divine favor, we would implore the Lord of Hosts to guide and direct our policy in the path of right, duty, justice and mercy, to unite our hearts and our efforts for the defense of our dearest rights, to strengthen our weakness, crown our arms with success, and enable us to secure a speedy, just and honorable peace.[22]

Lincoln displayed more humility:

It is peculiarly fit for us to recognize the hand of God in this terrible visitation, and in sorrowful remembrance of our own faults and crimes as a nation, and as individuals, to humble ourselves before Him and to pray for His mercy—to pray that we may be spared further punishment though most justly deserved; that our arms may be blessed and made effectual for the re-establishment of law, order, and peace throughout the wide extent of our country; and that the inestimable boon of civic and religious liberty, earned under His guidance and blessing by the labors and sufferings of our fathers, may be restored in all its original excellence.[23]

Thus both sides were going forth in the name of liberty and righteousness. Chaplains were appointed to all regiments. In the Confederate armies certain of the generals were noted for their piety. Soldiers' prayer meetings and revivals were of frequent occurrence. In the Union army the United States Christian Commission was organized and active. Many a Testament and tract was distributed and religious services were conducted regularly. The people themselves, already accustomed to the frequency of death, watched the newspapers for the black-bordered lists of the slain. The fellowship of suffering provided active ministration to the grief-stricken. Funeral marches and ballads of sorrow were composed and became part of the nation's grief: " Just Before the Battle, Mother "; " The Vacant Chair "; " All Quiet Along the Potomac Tonight "; " Somebody's Darling "; " Tenting Tonight on the Old Camp Ground." At length the delayed decision to emancipate the slaves stirred up even greater moral fervor and emphasized the belief that great moral issues were at stake, that it was a holy war on both sides for the preservation of something sacred.

The struggle in fact was a conflict and a confusing one, morally speaking, not between right and wrong but between two rights. As Lincoln phrased it:

> Both read the same Bible, and pray to the same God, and each invokes His aid against the other . . . . The prayers of both could not be answered. That of neither has been answered fully. The Almighty has His own purposes. "Woe unto the world because of offenses; for it must needs be that offenses come, but woe to

that man by whom the offense cometh." If . . . He gives to both North and South this terrible war, as the woe due to those by whom the offense came, shall we discern therein any departure from those Divine attributes which the believers in a living God always ascribe to Him? Fondly do we hope, fervently do we pray, that this mighty scourge of war may speedily pass away. Yet if God wills that it continue . . . as was said three thousand years ago, so still it must be said, "the judgments of the Lord are true and righteous altogether."

With malice toward none; with charity for all; with firmness in the right as God gives us to see the right, let us strive on to finish the work we are in, to bind up the nation's wounds, to care for him who shall have borne the battle, and for his widow, and his orphan, to do all which may achieve and cherish a just and lasting peace among ourselves, and with all nations.[24]

A month later Jefferson Davis, though Richmond had fallen and he was in flight, was declaring he would "die in the last ditch," never yielding to despondency. Relying upon the "never failing mercies and protecting care of our God," he called upon his countrymen "to meet the foe with fresh defiance, and unconquered and unconquerable hearts." [25]

The nation emerged from the conflict of the 1860's with a sense of having striven for something holy. Some thought of it as liberty, freedom, the Union. In the South there was hereafter to be the Lost Cause, the cause of self-government. In either case it was a great sacrifice made for the salvation of men. While some would be compelled to sing:

> Furl that Banner for 'tis weary, . . .
> Furl it, fold it, it is best . . .
> Furl it, hide it, let it rest.

yet others would raise the triumphant chorus, " Glory, Glory Hallelujah, Our God is Marching On."

The close of this chapter in the history of the association of religion and democracy did not end the book. The great era of big business which was to follow, which produced the concentration of wealth and power in the hands of multi-millionaires and giant corporations, only introduced a new stimulus to the moral imperative. This gigantic achievement appeared to have been accomplished at the expense of many who were poor and unfortunate. It was an era of debt and falling income for farmers, and they felt they were being exploited, even enslaved, by the railroads, middle men, bankers, manufacturers, and merchants joined in a larcenous conspiracy. Likewise, wage workers found themselves in an age of inflation falling into a species of wage slavery. Instead of independent farmers and master workmen, rural and urban proletariats seemed to be forming through the years with less and less hope and confidence.

The American Dream was proving an illusion except to a relatively few enterprisers. The genius of Evil was again seen at its nefarious work, through the Wolves of Wall Street, wicked men without conscience, motivated only by greed. Gold was the sign of their iniquity. Greenbacks and Free Silver became the emblems of man's salvation. The high point in this struggle for righteousness was William Jennings Bryan's thrilling peroration, "You shall not press down upon the brow of labor this crown of thorns. You shall not crucify mankind upon a cross of gold."

The crusade to work out the freedom of the farmer and the wage worker in terms of paper currency and silver coin failed, and the power of the Trusts grew. A new contest against evil was launched. A new prophet, Theodore Roosevelt, denounced Malefactors of Great Wealth and sought to invoke the power of government to examine business, not for the purpose of destroying all giant corporations, but in order to pass judgment, to divide them into "good" trusts and "bad" trusts, and to destroy those that were evil. He carried this contest for morality to the point that he led a new party singing "Onward Christian Soldiers" and proclaiming "We stand at Armageddon and we battle for the Lord." This was but prelude for the New Freedom of Woodrow Wilson, son of a Presbyterian clergyman.

The enthusiastic politics of the Muckrakers in the Progressive Era gave ample proof of one of the great truths of our democratic practice; namely, that those in political life who win the widest acclaim are generally those who are striving for reform. The generations who were descended from those seeking better things in a new world or from those more recently trained in the ideas and ideals above described could do no less than applaud those who demanded a return to righteousness. This spirit carried the nation on through two World Wars and the Great Depression.

It was in this spirit that Woodrow Wilson led America into war because of his belief that " the world must be made safe for democracy " and that " God helping her, she can do no other." It was in this spirit that Franklin D. Roosevelt sought divine blessing, protection, and guidance for himself and his countrymen in the war against fear, in his effort to drive the money-changers from the temple, in his striving to restore vision to the people lest they perish, and finally in the crusade to preserve the Four Freedoms. It was in this spirit that Dwight D. Eisenhower opened his administration with a prayer of his own uttering.

And now in this troubled day of the present, citizens of the United States summon once again this century-old sense of dedication and moral purpose to aid them as they combat the enemy within and without. The rise and tactics of Communist leadership compel the nation to realize that its citizens are in the midst of a conflict of ideologies and of a contest between the Soviets and the western powers in which American democracy is fully committed to a battle which at times involves it in confusion. Once again there are pleas to defend the faith, to make strong and invincible the holy cause of democracy. To the inspired sight of many there is still the vision glorious, but it has competition.

Today Americans find themselves the heirs of three centuries and a half of special experience, an experience most intimately connected in unique fashion with man's deepest religious emotions. This experience has had an influence upon all which is unmeasurable and largely unrecognized; but so strong is it that, if Americans fail to realize it, they walk forward blindly deprived of a great light which is truly theirs. If they are to grasp its significance and profit by its strength they will do well to look backward and trace the incidents of this experience.

The people of the United States may well remember that there was a time in simpler days when governments were held to be holy, ordained by God to work His purposes among men just as was His church. There is no longer the close union of church and state in much of the western world, but this separation in the American democracy has never eliminated the influence of basic religious concepts or moral imperatives.

It may be profitably maintained that it would be in the interest of the general welfare if American citizens could continue to hold their rights and responsibilities of self-government as sacred, that those to whom the duties of government be entrusted should feel that theirs is a trust to be carried out in a spirit of democratic dedication, that they should believe that the purity of government is of the highest concern to society. Neither religion nor government should ever be taken for granted. If they are, if there is merely a vague faith but no living zeal for the cause of liberty and self-government, it will wither and may even die.

The nation, however, is fortunate in the fact that it has this great tradition recorded in the form of the utterances of so many leaders. This wisdom, this scriptural literature, is always before us and will be handed on by the nation's spokesmen. This moral imperative has become a part of American culture, a directive which inspires faith and promotes right conduct. It may well insure American salvation in that it resembles religion. But, like religion, American Democracy has at least two components, fear and faith. Man fears evil but has faith to believe that he may be protected or may protect himself against that which he fears. In their most effective combination this fear and this faith produce the courage and the capacity for effective action which enable men to overcome evil and achieve righteousness.

This the American nation must have faith to believe that democracy can do—that it can create a way of life and maintain a form of government which will enable its people to live by these principles of justice and charity, which will permit each individual self-government to the limit of his ability. Democracy is not easy. There is the danger that the fear component may undermine the faith component; and instead of courage and capacity, generate bigotry, intolerance, and the cruel suppression of individual dignity and competence. Such an outcome would in the end destroy the truly religious quality of democracy and transform it into a degrading tyranny.

A true dedication to righteousness dispels darkness, rather than intensifies it; it does not destroy, it creates. It is the great creator of faith, hope, and charity. Over the centuries America's growing population has been so largely motivated by faith and hope that it has achieved probably a greater measure of charity than is the general characteristic of human societies. The nation should find in this experience a cumulative moral imperative commanding that it continue to follow these patterns. Americans will be able to do so only if they continue to have faith that they can. It is one of the lessons of human experience that faith creates the power necessary to accomplish that which men believe should be done. However, loss of faith destroys the will and the power to achieve. Only if Americans continue to believe that they should maintain their democracy in its purity can their faith make it possible for them to generate the needed strength. This, then, must be their faith, their dedication to maintain American democracy.

In the beginning of this consideration American democracy was presented as being constructed at a time when man as an individual was emerging from the mass of mankind and finding himself as a person. This experience was closely connected with religion. Now when there are so many influences at work to drive man back into the mass, shorn of his individuality, this belief in democracy, if maintained with religious fervor, may be the saving agent which will keep him still an individual, strong in his faith, in his dignity, and in his power derived from his religious insight. Man's belief in his capacity for self-government under divine guidance may well be the salvation of the American Way.

NOTES TO THE TEXT

NOTES TO PART I

[1] E. G. Rupp, *Studies in the Making of the English Protestant Tradition* (Cambridge, England, 1949), 1-46; Roy F. Nichols, "English Origins of American Politics," *Pennsylvania Magazine of History and Biography*, LXXVI, 5-29.

[2] Andrew L. Drummond, *Story of American Protestantism* (Boston, 1951), 50-51.

[3] Henry Steele Commager (ed.), *Documents of American History* (2nd. ed.; New York, 1940), 15-16.

[4] Drummond, *Story of American Protestantism*, 49.

[5] Samuel Eliot Morison, *Builders of the Bay Colony* (Boston, 1930), 64.

[6] Commager (ed.), *Documents of American History*, 18.

[7] *Ibid.*

[8] Morison, *Builders of the Bay Colony*, 71.

[9] Commager (ed.), *Documents of American History*, 23.

[10] William Macdonald (ed.), *Documentary Source Book of American History, 1606-1926* (3rd ed.; New York, 1926), 40-43.

[11] "Records of the Town of Newark, New Jersey," in *Collections of the New Jersey Historical Society* (Newark, N. J., 1864), VI, 1-4.

[12] *Remember William Penn, 1644-1944*, Prepared by the Editorial Committee of the William Penn Tercentenary Committee (Harrisburg, Pa., 1944), 60.

[13] William W. Comfort, *William Penn, 1644-1718, A Tercentenary Estimate* (Philadelphia, 1944), 136.

[14] *Remember William Penn, 1644-1944*, 77.

[15] *Ibid.*, 85.

[16] *William Penn, 1644-1718*, p. 141.

[17] Commager (ed.), *Documents of American History*, 8-10.

[18] *Ibid.*, 100-102.

[19] *Ibid.*, 115.

[20] *Ibid.*, 145.

[21] James D. Richardson (ed.), *A Compilation of the Messages and Papers of the Presidents* (Washington, 1899), I, 52-54.

[22] *Ibid.*, 55.

[23] *Ibid.*, 56.

[24] *Ibid.*, 55.

[25] *Ibid.*, 64.

[26] *Ibid.*, 65.

[27] Edward G. Bourne, *Spain in America* (New York, 1904), 47-48.

[28] Herbert E. Bolton, *Wider Horizons of American History* (New York, 1939), 146-47.

NOTES TO PART II

[1] Timothy L. Smith, *Revivalism and Social Reform in Mid-Nineteenth-Century America* (New York, 1957), 35.

[2] Isaac Watts, *Songs Divine and Moral, For the Use of Children* (Boston, n. d.), 29.

[3] *Little Susy's Little Servants by Her Aunt Susan*, First Series (New York, 1866), 109-110.

[4] *The Deserter* (American Tract Society: New York, n. d.), 10.

[5] Lynde Palmer, *Helps Over Hard Places: Stories for Girls* (Boston, 1862), vii.

[6] Theodore Thinker, *The A. B. C. Picture Book* (New York, 1853), 94-96.

[7] S. F. Smith (ed.), *Lyric Gems* (Boston, 1844), 94.

[8] Jacob Abbott, *The Young Christian* . . . (New York, 1833), 24.

[9] Daniel Wise, *The Young Man's Counsellor* . . . (New York, 1850), 40-42.

[10] David Magie, *The Spring-Time of Life* (New York, 1855), 26-28.

[11] Isaac Watts, *The Improvement of the Mind* . . . (Boston, 1793), 4.

[12] Lindley Murray, *The English Reader* . . . (Ithaca, N. Y., 1826), 17-18.

[13] Mrs. Phelps, *Natural Philosophy for Beginners* . . . (New York, 1839), 13.

[14] T. H. Gallaudet, *The Youth's Book on Natural Theology* (New York, 1832), 8-9.

[15] [Samuel G. Goodrich,] *Peter Parley's Common School History* (Philadelphia, 1847), 288-89.

[16] *Lady's Almanac for the Year 1858* (Boston [1857]), 64.

[17] Commager (ed.), *Documents of American History*, 373-74.

[18] James D. Richardson (ed.), *A Compilation of the Messages and Papers of the Confederacy* (Nashville, Tenn., 1905), I, 36.

[19] *Idem, Messages and Papers of the Presidents*, VI, 11.

[20] *Idem, Messages and Papers of the Confederacy*, I, 82.

[21] *Idem, Messages and Papers of the Presidents*, VI, 31.

[22] *Idem, Messages and Papers of the Confederacy*, I, 103.

[23] *Idem, Messages and Papers of the Presidents*, VI, 36.

[24] *Ibid.*, VI, 276-77.

[25] Richardson (ed.), *Messages and Papers of the Confederacy*, I, 569-70.

BIBLIOGRAPHICAL SUGGESTIONS

A. DOCUMENTS

Comfort, William W. *William Penn, 1644-1718, A Tercentenary Estimate.* Philadelphia, 1944.
A Compilation of the Messages and Papers of the Confederacy. Edited by James D. Richardson. Nashville, 1905.
A Compilation of the Messages and Papers of the Presidents. Edited by James D. Richardson. Washington, 1899.
Documents of American History. Edited by Henry Steele Commager. 2nd. ed. New York, 1940.
Documentary Source Book of American History, 1606-1926. Edited by William Macdonald. 3rd. ed. New York, 1926.
" Records of the Town of Newark, New Jersey," *Collections of the New Jersey Historical Society,* Vol. VI. Newark, 1864.
Remember William Penn, 1644-1944. Prepared by Editorial Committee of the William Penn Tercentenary Committee. Harrisburg,1944.

B. CONTEMPORARY TRACTS

Abbott, Jacob. *The Young Christian, or, A Familiar Illustration of the Principles of Christian Duty.* New York, 1833.
The Deserter. American Tract Society: New York, n. d.
Gallaudet, T. H. *The Youth's Book on Natural Theology.* New York, 1832.
[Goodrich, Samuel G.]. *Peter Parley's Common School History.* Philadelphia, 1847.
Kiefer, Monica Mary. *American Children Through Their Books, 1700-1835.* Philadelphia, 1948.
Lady's Almanac for the Year 1858. Boston, [1857].

Little Susy's Little Servants by Her Aunt Susan. First Series. New York, 1866.

Lyric Gems. Edited by S. F. Smith. Boston, 1844.

Magie, David. *The Spring-Time of Life; or, Advice to Youth*. New York, 1855.

Murray, Lindley. *The English Reader; or, Pieces in Prose and Poetry, from the Best Writers; designed to assist young persons to Read with Propriety and Effect, improve their language and sentiments; and to inculcate the most important principles of Piety and Virtue with a few preliminary Observations on the Principles of Good Reading*. Ithaca, 1826.

Palmer, Lynde. *Helps Over Hard Places: Stories for Girls*. Boston, 1862.

Phelps, Mrs. *Natural Philosophy for Beginners; Designed for Common Schools and Families*. New York, 1839.

Thinker, Theodore. *The A. B. C. Picture Book*. New York, 1853.

Watts, Isaac. *The Improvement of the Mind; or, A Supplement to the Art of Logic . . . to which is added a Discourse on the Education of Children and Youth*. Boston, 1793.

———. *Songs, Divine and Moral, for the Use of Children*. Boston, n. d.

Wise, Daniel. *The Young Man's Counsellor; or, Sketches and Illustrations of the Duties and Dangers of Young Men—Designed to be a Guide to Success in this Life, and to Happiness in the Life which is to come*. New York, 1850.

C. SELECTED GENERAL STUDIES

Barnes, Gilbert H. *The Anti-Slavery Impulse*. New York, 1933.

Bennett, William W. *A narrative of the great revival which prevailed in the Southern armies during the late Civil*

War between the States of the Federal Union. Philadelphia, 1877.

Bolton, Herbert E. *Wider Horizons of American History.* New York, 1939.

Bourne, Edward G. *Spain in America.* New York, 1904.

Cole, Charles C., Jr. *Social Ideas of the Northern Evangelists, 1826-1860.* New York, 1954.

Cross, Whitney R. *The Burned-over District: The Social and Intellectual History of Enthusiastic Religion in Western New York, 1800-1850.* Ithaca, 1950.

Drummond, Andrew L. *Story of American Protestantism.* Boston, 1951.

Francis, Russell E. " Pentecost: 1858. A Study in Religious Revivals." Unpublished Ph. D. dissertation, University of Pennsylvania, 1948.

Gaustad, Edwin S. *The Great Awakening in New England.* New York, 1957.

Horton, Douglas. *Congregationalism, A Study in Church Polity.* London, 1952.

Hudson, Winthrop S. *Great Tradition of the American Churches.* New York, 1953.

Jenkins, Daniel T. *Tradition, Freedom and the Spirit.* Philadelphia, 1952.

Jones, John W. *Christ in the Camp; or, Religion in Lee's Army.* Richmond, 1887.

Koch, Gustav A. *Republican Religion: The American Revolution and the Cult of Reason.* New York, 1933.

Maynard, Theodore. *Story of American Catholicism.* New York, 1941.

Miller, Perry. *Errand into the Wilderness.* Cambridge, Mass., 1956.

————. *Jonathan Edwards.* New York, 1949.

————. *Orthodoxy in Massachusetts.* Massachusetts, 1933.

————. *New England Mind.* Massachusetts, 1939.

Miller, Perry, and T. H. Johnson (eds.). *Puritans.* New York, 1938.

Morey, Verne D. "American Congregationalism: A Critical Bibliography, 1900-1952," *Church History,* XXI (December, 1952), 323-44.

Morison, Samuel Eliot. *Builders of the Bay Colony.* Boston, 1930.

Nichols, Roy F. "English Origins of American Politics," *Pennsylvania Magazine of History and Biography,* LXXVI (January, 1952), 5-29.

Priestley, Herbert I. *The Coming of the White Man, 1492-1848.* New York, 1929.

Rupp, E. G. *Studies in the Making of the English Protestant Tradition.* Cambridge, England, 1949.

Silver, James W. *Confederate Morale and Church Propaganda.* Tuscaloosa, 1957.

Smith, Timothy L. *Revivalism and Social Reform in Mid-Nineteenth-Century America.* New York, 1957.

Sweet, William W. *Revivalism in America.* New York, 1945.

Thompson, Charles L. *Times of Refreshing: A History of American Revivals from 1740 to 1877.* Chicago, 1877.

Trinterud, Leonard J. *The Forming of an American Tradition.* Philadelphia, 1949.

261.70973
N62   **Date Due**